THE POETRY OF THE CELTIC RACES.

KENNIKAT PRESS SCHOLARLY REPRINTS
Ralph Adams Brown, Senior Editor

Series In
IRISH HISTORY AND CULTURE
Under the General Editorial Supervision of
Gilbert A. Cahill
Professor of History, State University of New York

The Poetry of the Celtic Races, and other Studies by Ernest Renan.

Translated, with Introduction and Notes, by William G. Hutchison.

KENNIKAT PRESS
Port Washington, N. Y./London

THE POETRY OF THE CELTIC RACES,
AND OTHER STUDIES

First published in 1896
Reissued in 1970 by Kennikat Press
Library of Congress Catalog Card No: 74-102627
SBN 8046-0803-2

Manufactured by Taylor Publishing Company Dallas, Texas

KENNIKAT SERIES IN IRISH HISTORY AND CULTURE

CONTENTS.

INTRODUCTION.

In the history of modern European thought there are few more interesting contrasts, than that which results from a consideration of the attitude of the eighteenth and the nineteenth century sceptic towards popular beliefs and superstitions. If we further limit our view to France, and further still, to two French men of letters, each of whom fitly represents his own epoch, the contrast, in that it is focussed into smaller compass, is perhaps the more striking. Voltaire and Renan have at least one thing in common: each of them in his time was the *bête noire* of his orthodox contemporaries, each of them was proclaimed to be the Antichrist foretold of old. The name of Voltaire to this day brings a shudder to many worthy persons, while Renan's *Life of Jesus* caused the publication, in France alone, of fifteen hundred controversial books and pamphlets within a year of its publication. But they are sceptics with a difference: Voltaire's opinion of dogmatic and theocratic Christianity—so far as one can gather that remarkable man's real opinion of anything—was summed up in his well-known phrase, "*Écrasez l'Infame!*" "I wish you," he wrote to D'Alembert in 1760, "to crush the Infamous One—that is the great point." Renan was an iconoclast of another type. He always retained a profound veneration for the simple religious life in which his childhood and youth had been passed. He had left it with regret, and had kept, if not the form, much of the spirit of the old faith. "Simple faith," he says, "is the true faith; and I confess that I should be inconsolable, if I learned that my writings had scandalised one of those folk of childlike soul who so truly worship in spirit."[1] Where Voltaire could only find cause for a burst of brilliant raillery, Renan sees something to be treated with a gentle and loving touch; Voltaire's mocking laughter becomes a barely perceptible smile, and his pitiless analysis a sympathetic synthesis. Both Voltaire and Renan are critics; but the former attacks, the latter explains, and in so doing proves himself to be the greater critic of the twain. For the critic *par excellence* neither concludes nor excludes; his aim is to understand without believing, to find other people's enthusiasm useful and suggestive without sharing it, above all to have a mind free from illusion. In fairness it must be added however that, if Voltaire's scepticism tends ever towards cynicism, that of Renan sometimes approaches perilously close to undue sensibility, the sensibility that delights in feeding upon the religious emotion of the orthodox, without feeling bound to pay for the pleasure by an affirmation of its legitimacy.

[1] *Études d'Histoire Religieuse.*

We can account, in some measure, for the difference in attitude between Voltaire and Renan by the product-of-the-century theory, of which Taine and Sainte-Beuve were so greatly enamoured. But I am inclined to lay more stress upon the influence of heredity and early environment. Voltaire was a Parisian by birth, and most essentially French in temperament; Renan was a Breton. It would be a somewhat forced application of a well-worn phrase to say, that if you scratch Renan you find a Breton. At the same time, too much importance cannot be attached to the fact that beneath his Gallicism, with its brilliant wit and genius for critical analysis, there lay a deep substratum of the Celtic spirit, its naïve intuition, its romanticism, its dreamy idealism. Through his mother he inherited a strain of Gascon blood; his father was a pure Breton.

Joseph Ernest Renan was born on February 28th, 1823, at Tréguier, a little town in Brittany. He came of a race of seafarers, and, in all probability, was a descendant of St. Renan (or Ronan), one of the migrants who in great numbers came to Brittany from Wales and Ireland during the fifth century. Renan's parents were of humble position; they had two means of subsistence, the one a small coasting-vessel, the other a little "general" shop. But they had a hard fight to make ends meet—the Renans were traditionally unable to save money—and at last, when Ernest was a child of five, the climax of the family misfortunes was reached. One dark night the father in going back to his ship, fell from the quay at St. Malo and was drowned. He left the family deeply in debt, but the creditors accepted an offer made by Ernest's sister, Henriette, then a girl of fifteen, to pay off her father's debts by degrees. This she accomplished after twenty years of labour and sacrifice. She began by keeping an infant school, and, finding it successful, she settled at Lannion, a town of more importance than Tréguier. However, convent schools began to spring up, Henriette's academy was abandoned for lack of pupils, and the Renans returned to Tréguier. And then Ernest's education began. The good sister and a cousin in the priesthood paid his first school-fees, but he soon relieved them of the burden by gaining a scholarship in the ecclesiastical seminary of the town. He was a model pupil, studious, docile, and of great piety; indeed, his rather un-boyish qualities earned him the nickname of "Mademoiselle," and much teasing from his less effeminate schoolfellows. He ever retained an affectionate memory of the old priests who were his earliest preceptors. Narrow their ideas might be, but they were good and honourable men, and they honestly strove to instil their own simple virtues into the minds of their pupils. Another portrait of this period of Renan's life which he depicts with tender art is that of the beautiful little girl, Noémi, whom he loved, child as he was, and after whom in latter years he named his first-born daughter. Renan's boyhood in Brittany, that land of desolate moors and grey skies, was an education in romanticism. Tréguier itself, with its convents and ancient cathedral, a survival of the ages of faith and ecclesiasticism; the surrounding country, dotted with little chapels of local saints unknown to the rest of Christendom—Tudwal, and Iltud, and a hundred more; old churchyards fronting the grey sea—which covers, so the Breton legend tells, the city of Is, whose spires may be seen in the hollow of the waves when the sea is rough, whose bells can be heard pealing when the day is calm and still:—such was the scene of Renan's early years, and it left indelible impressions on his memory and his temperament.

At the age of fifteen a great change came over Renan's life, but for which he would have probably spent the remainder of it as a country *curé*, or perhaps as a professor of theology in the College of Tréguier. The Abbé Dupanloup, whose successful conversion of Talleyrand had given him fame in the Catholic circles of France, was in 1838 at the head of a great ecclesiastical preparatory school in Paris—St. Nicolas du Chardonnet. His pupils were recruited in two ways. He had under his charge many boys belonging to aristocratic families. From these he received large fees; and this enabled him to give a gratuitous education to boys of poor birth but exceptional ability. To obtain the latter the Abbé used to send emissaries to different parts of France. Renan fell under the notice of one of these recruiting-agents, when, in the year 1838, he had won all the prizes of his class in the Tréguier College. A summons from the Abbé reached him during his summer vacation, and in three days he was in Paris. "This was the gravest crisis of my life," he writes in his *Souvenirs*;[1] "the young Breton does not bear trans-

[1] *Souvenirs d'Enfance et de Jeunesse* (1883).

planting. The keen moral repulsion which I felt, added to a complete change in my habits and mode of life, brought on a very severe attack of home-sickness." So severe indeed was his home-sickness, that he became seriously ill, almost to the point of death. "I sometimes think that the Breton part of me did die; the Gascon unfortunately found sufficient reason for living. The latter discovered too, that this new world was a very curious one, and was well worth clinging to."[1]

St. Nicolas was an establishment of two hundred students, and it was scarcely to be expected that its busy superintendent should at once take a personal interest in the new-comer. But a connecting link was established between the Abbé and the home-sick boy. The former had a mother whom he held in tender affection, and one of Renan's letters to his own dearly-loved mother fell into his hands. "Thenceforward he took notice of me. He recognised my existence, and he was for me what he was for all of us—a principle of life, a sort of deity."[1] This mental forcing-house of St. Nicolas was the means of introducing Renan to a new world of ideas. For his old Breton teachers, literature had ended with the Revolution; but here in Paris the Romantic movement was at its height, *Hernani* had been produced a few years previously, and Hugo and Lamartine became his intellectual stimulants.

Once more however he was to pass into a new atmosphere. From St. Nicolas, where rhetoric and literature were the chief subjects of study, he entered

[1] *Souvenirs.*

the branch establishment, at Issy, of the Theological Seminary of St. Sulplice, where he studied philosophy—or at least such of it as had obtained the sanction of the Church—and devoted much time and meditation to Descartes, Pascal, Malebranche, and other philosophers, including Reid and the Scottish school. These two years at Issy were only a preparation for St. Sulplice, where his studies were divided into two parts—dogmatics and moral philosophy. Theological and philosophical teaching formed one great whole, the smallest detail of which could not be removed without danger. In connection with the theological side of this system of education, it was necessary to study the Bible in the original languages; and, under the guidance of Le Hir, a man of accomplishment and learning, Renan threw himself into this part of his work with unbounded enthusiasm. He soon made great progress in the study of the Semitic languages; and, since an acquaintance with the great German critics and philologists was indispensable to him, he learned German. Le Hir also had a profound knowledge of the methods and results of German exegesis, but his orthodoxy was unshaken and indeed unshakable. Renan describes him as a man whose mind was divided into water-tight compartments; and probably had he himself possessed a mind of like construction, he would have ended his days as a bishop in the odour of sanctity.

But it was not to be so. Even before leaving Issy slight signs of scepticism had been apparent in Renan, though probably he was not at that time fully conscious of any approaching crisis. One of the Issy professors had indeed roundly charged him with infidelity; but his agony of remorse had been gently healed by the Principal of the establishment, who had a comfortable theory that a young man's theological doubts were somewhat of the nature of a distemper, which would pass away in due course. But Renan's scepticism was not a passing phase. His studies in German philosophy had given him a wider outlook on the world of ideas, than is desirable for a young man who intends to become a Roman Catholic priest; above all, his Semitic studies convinced him that inspiration, as the Church conceived it, was out of the question, and that the Bible must bear the same critical treatment as any other great literature. He came to recognise the fallacy of the circular argument employed by dogmatic Catholicism:—the infallibility of the Church rests on that of the Bible, but then the infallibility of the Bible rests on that of the Church. Now whether, as we are repeatedly assured, neither Catholic nor Protestant is bound up with the infallibility of the Bible, whether a man may be an orthodox Catholic or Protestant without such a belief, Renan held strongly to the opinion that the faith of his Church was tied to literal inspiration, and had no respect for the religious trimmer in his attempts towards reconciling the irreconcilable. The true Catholic, he said, would be inflexible in the declaration: "If I must abandon my past, I shall abandon the whole; for I believe in everything upon the principle of infallibility, and the principle is as much affected by one small concession as by ten thousand large ones."[1] It was then Biblical and historical criticism that did most to shake his positive faith. Such *a priori* convictions as he had were always vague; at this period of his life they were theistic in tendency, and for a time indeed his mind was drawn, mainly by the influence of Herder's writings, towards rationalistic Protestantism. Though outwardly he was still a devout Christian, taking part in all the duties and services of the Church, a fierce conflict was being waged within him. In his twenty-third year he stood at the parting of the ways. Was he to go on in his present path, and teach all his life dogmas in which he had ceased to believe? Or was he to break off everything, at the risk of causing pain to his preceptors and his gentle, pious mother? Honesty bade him pursue the latter course; and his sister Henriette, who was now a governess in Poland, strongly advised him not to bind himself over to the Church, promised to find him a tutorship, and sent him £40 with which to support himself for the time. At last the crisis came. Arriving at St. Sulplice in the autumn of 1845 from his annual holiday in Brittany, he learned that he had been appointed to a Carmelite institution in Paris. He at once refused the appointment, and had an interview with his former Principal, the Abbé Dupanloup, who told him very decisively that he had no right to remain in the Church a day longer. He also offered him pecuniary assistance, but this, owing to Henriette's generous action, was unnecessary.

[1] *Souvenirs.*

On the 6th of October 1845, Renan left St. Sulplice, and commenced upon a new chapter in his life. From his *Souvenirs* one can learn how long and bitter was the strife that ended thus.

"Because a Parisian *gamin* disposes with a jest of creeds from which Pascal, with all his reasoning powers, could not shake himself free, it must not be concluded that the *gamin* is superior to Pascal. I confess that at times I feel humiliated to think that it cost me five or six years of arduous research, and the study of Hebrew, the Semitic languages, Gesenius, and Ewald, to arrive at the result which this urchin achieves in a twinkling. . . . But Père Hardouin used to say that he had not got up at four o'clock every morning for forty years, to think as all the world thought. So I am loth to admit that I have been at so much pains to fight a mere *Chimæra bombinans*. . . . There are in reality but few people who have a right to disbelieve in Christianity." To support himself in his new life, Renan accepted a post as tutor in an educational boarding-house, where he received board and lodgings in return for his services. These duties were light, and most of his time was given to study, to passing examinations, and to writing for periodicals; and naturally philology, more especially that of the Semitic languages, claimed the greater part of his attention. At this time too he made the acquaintance of a man who was destined to be his life-long friend—Marcellin Berthelot, the distinguished chemist and statesman. The friendship of two men of intellectual genius can never be unfruitful of result, both for themselves and for the world at large; and that of Renan and Berthelot was no exception to the rule. Though their paths were different, each was interested in the work of the other (Renan sometimes regretted that he had not devoted himself to physical science); and together they discussed interminably the great problems that lie beyond all science, and up to which all scientific thought inevitably leads. How great was Berthelot's influence may be gathered from Renan's work, *The Future of Science*, which was written in 1848, but remained unpublished for another forty years. In this curious book Renan first set down his general ideas of the universe. He described, in his forecast of things to be, a world where, as in Plato's Republic, philosophy would be on the throne, where the religious wants of men would be met by culture, and "the beautiful and passionate quest of truth." This state of society was to be attained, not by an equable redistribution of material wealth, but by the universal diffusion of the "sweetness and light" of humanism. In its enthusiastic conviction of tone and certitude, it is pre-eminently the work of a young man; but its general ideas always remained the fundamental base of nearly all his later thought.

The year 1847 saw Renan's first appearance in the world of science and letters as the winner of the Volney prize at the Institute of France. His prize essay, afterwards developed into a *General History of the Semitic Languages*, gained him the friendship of Eugène Bournouf, who was then Professor of Sanscrit at the College of France; and he commenced to attend the latter's lectures, thereby adding to his knowledge of the Semitic languages a profound acquaintance with Indian literature and mythology. Renan had by this time attracted sufficient attention for the Académie des Inscriptions et Belles-Lettres to send him on a literary mission to Italy; and the successful manner in which he carried out and reported on his labours led to his appointment, in 1851, to a post in the Bibliothèque Nationale, and, in 1856, to membership of the Académie des Inscriptions et Belles-Lettres. In the meantime he had published his work on Averroes, the philosopher of Mohammedan Spain, and the *General History of the Semitic Languages* already mentioned.

His means were now almost sufficient to permit him to marry the woman of his choice, Cornélie Scheffer, niece of the famous painter of that name. His sister, who had been keeping house for him, came to the aid of the young people, and, with characteristic generosity, enabled them to commence their married life. Renan's was a very happy marriage, and his household of course included Henriette. Many of his contributions to the *Revue des Deux Mondes* and the *Journal des Débats* were now collected and published in *Études d'Histoire Religieuse* (1857) and *Essais de Morale et de Critique* (1859). Perhaps more than any other man of his time, Renan executed a double programme of intellectual labour. On the one hand, he was constantly engaged on the principal work of his life—the history of the Semitic tongues, of the early Christian Church, and of the People of Israel; on the other, he was ever ready to turn his attention to contemporary thought and action. In these two volumes the range of his subjects is very great: Mohammed and Channing, Calvin and Lamennais, the Religions of Antiquity and the Poetry of the Celtic Races—all these indicate the breadth of his learning, and his genius for exposition. He appeals to us as a philologist, a historian, a theologian, and a literary critic. And to each of these characters is added that of the man of letters, who, of whatever subject he may treat, endows it with the crowning gift of style. One of the most interesting essays in the *Études* is that on the "Critical Historians of Jesus," interesting because it foreshadows his own much discussed work. He gives special attention to Strauss, whose first biography of Jesus had been published in 1835, and gives him high praise, qualified, however, by criticism of his tendency to dissociate the events of the life of Jesus from actual occurrences, and of his too close adherence to Hegelian thought. An essay from each of these two books appears in the present volume. That from *Études*, on Feuerbach, is chiefly valuable for the light it throws upon Renan's view of Christianity, and upon his intense dislike of the dogmatic atheism of which Feuerbach—who has become somewhat of an extinct volcano—was such a doughty champion. The beautiful essay on the Poetry of the Celtic Races shows Renan at his best. What more congenial theme could he find than the poetry of mystery and romantic imagination, which has been given to the world by his own race, that race which he knew and loved so well? It was to the legends, the poetry, the religion of his boyhood, to his own forefathers, to St. Renan and Peredur, to St. Brandan and St. Patrick, that he devoted some of his most delicate criticism and most impassioned prose. I cannot refrain from quoting from the preface—

"O fathers of the obscure tribe by whose fireside I drank in faith in the unseen, humble clan of workers and mariners to whom I owe the vigour of my soul in an exhausted land, in an age when hope is dead,—I doubt not that you wandered over those enchanted seas where our father Brandan sought the Land of Promise, that you gazed upon those green isles whose grass dipped in the waves, that with St. Patrick you traversed the circle of that world no longer beheld of the eyes of men. . . Let us be consoled by our fantasies, by our nobility, by our disdain. Who knows but that those dreams are truer than reality? God be my witness, ancient fathers, that my only delight lies in this—that at times I feel that I am your conscience, that through me you attain life and utterance."

Renan's studies in Semitic literature had hitherto been principally addressed to the *savant* and the specialist. In 1859 he appealed to a wider public by publishing a new translation of the Book of Job. Renan's own prose so often trespasses on the domain of poetry, that it is scarcely necessary to speak of the beauty of his rendering. In the following year he followed up the poem of Job, with its despairing defiance of destiny and its atmosphere of gloom, by publishing a new edition of one of the most idyllic and human poems of the Bible—the Song of Songs. Like Ewald, he of course dismisses the fruitless attempts, which have been made since the days of Philo and Origen, to force an allegorical interpretation on the poem. Like Ewald also, he re-arranges the somewhat incoherent text in which it appears in the ordinary versions, so as to give it the form of a lyrical drama.

By this time Renan's reputation as an Oriental scholar was firmly established, and in 1860 Napoleon III. asked him to undertake an expedition to Phœnicia, for the purpose of examining ancient sites in that country. Renan accepted the invitation, and set out in company with his wife and sister. The former soon returned to France, but Henriette remained with her brother till her death from fever in September 1861. She passed away while Renan, who had been attacked by the same disease, was lying unconscious. His grief on hearing of his loss was of the most poignant kind. None knew so well as himself all that he owed to Henriette, to her tender solicitude, her unselfishness, her unfailing love; and in a short biographical sketch—originally printed for private circulation—he told the story of her life. All who have read the *Life of Jesus* will remember the touching dedication, "To the pure soul of my Sister Henriette."

As is related in that dedication, he commenced, while in Syria, upon what was destined to be his best known work. It was not however finally completed and published until 1863, when it took the reading world by storm. It appealed principally of course to that rather wide circle of readers who, without having a belief in the supernatural side of religion, feel a dislike for the arid and negative teaching of eighteenth century deism and some modern forms of scepticism. To such as these Renan's new gospel appeared an honest attempt at bringing the life of the Founder of Christianity into the light of modern historical study; but, as might be expected, the publication of the work was, for orthodox opinion, as a match applied to a powder magazine. The air was darkened with the fifteen hundred books and pamphlets which their authors felt moved to launch at Renan's head, rumours of the most libellous kind about his private character were put in circulation, and an anonymous but pious lady sent him, during the rest of his life, a monthly letter containing a kindly reminder that there was a hell! It is not my intention to add appreciably to the mass of criticism, good, bad, and indifferent, which has clustered about the *Life of Jesus.* Whether or not it be an epoch-making book, one can at least confidently assert that it has had the profoundest influence on modern conceptions of the origin of Christianity. The absolutely impartial historian has never yet lived, and probably never will. Renan had his own *a priori* view of his subject, his own way of looking at events —if you will, his own prejudices. The moral beauty of Christian teaching he found in the gentleness, the mildness, the "sweet reasonableness" of Jesus; the intellectual beauty, in the idea of "the Kingdom of God." He has been accused of straining conjecture, of using romantic invention, of writing for effect, of being picturesque for the sake of being picturesque. But the same criticism could be applied to any historian with a great subject, a paucity of data, and an instinct for filling up gaps. The historian must be a creator as well as a critic; a great historian of no imagination is a contradiction in terms. And Renan's good faith is beyond question; the accumulation of references at the foot of his pages is sometimes overpowering; he is never polemical or unduly dogmatic. But the harmonious cadences of its exquisite prose, the perfection of its descriptions, the sweet seduction of its sentiment, need not blind us to the fact that this sentiment occasionally passes into sentimentalism, and that the æsthetic aspect of the subject is accorded an undue preponderance. The story goes that a certain lady having picked up the *Life of Jesus* was so fascinated, that she devoured it as though it were one of the most dramatic and enthralling of romances. With a sigh, not of relief but of insatiety, she read the final page and exclaimed: "What worries me is that it doesn't wind up with a wedding!"—*Ce qui m'ennuie c'est que cela ne finit pas par un mariage!* This anecdote indicates both the strength and the weakness of the book.

The clamours raised by its publication had, as one result, the final dismissal of Renan from the Chair of Hebrew, which he had occupied in the College of France since 1862. His inaugural lecture, by its prediction of the separation of Church and State, and by a passage in which the Founder of Christianity was called a man,[1] had set clerical influence at work in the Imperial Court and caused his suspension.

[1] The passage was as follows:—"A reform of Judaism, one so profound and so peculiar that it was in truth a complete creation, was achieved by a man, to whom no other man can be compared, a man so great

He had continued, however, to receive his salary, and to give private instruction to his students; but now, after a correspondence in which Renan showed dignity and a command of ironical wit, the appointment was formally revoked, and he found himself thrown on his own resources, by this time however, owing to his successes in literature, sufficient for his needs.

The Apostles were to form the subject of the next volume in the *History of the Origins of Christianity;* and in 1864 Renan set out on another Eastern tour, with the aim of visiting the localities which were to be the background of the book. *Les Apôtres* appeared in 1864, and was followed, three years later, by the volume devoted to St. Paul. To touch adequately on these and the succeeding volumes of the *Origins* would be out of place here, and I must therefore do no more than chronicle their appearance. Both religious and political subjects were treated in *Questions Contemporaines*, a volume published in 1868. Renan's mind was greatly exercised at this time by the critical state of French politics. The Emperor had fallen more and more under the influence of the clerical party, and, as an inevitable consequence, a retrogressive policy was adopted with regard to the Papal and other questions. In the general election of May 1869 Renan emerged from his study, and appeared in the political arena as a candidate. His political creed was that of a moderate liberal,

that, although in this place everything must be judged from the point of view of positive science, I should be loth to contradict those who, struck by the exceptional character of his work, call him God."

favouring reform, the development of public education, and freedom of association, religion, and the press, but averse to any violent or sudden changes. He was opposed by the two extreme parties, that of the Government, and that of the Republicans, and lost the day.

In the summer of the following year Renan made a tour in Scotland and the North of Europe with Prince Napoleon; but it was cut short by a telegram which reached them at Tromsöe, in Norway, and informed them that war with Germany was inevitable. The fateful news took them by surprise. To Renan the future of France had seemed likely to be melancholy and commonplace, but such a cataclysm as this he had not expected. He thought it the consequence of a sudden fit of insanity. A word or two concerning the well-known controversy with Strauss may be said here. A fortnight before the "*débacle*" of Sedan, but when the ultimate success of Germany was assured, the latter sent Renan a long letter in which, after a dissertation on the modern history of Europe, especially as it bore on French aggression and thirst for primacy, he administered to France through the medium of his correspondent a species of moral lecture on her natural failings, and, naturally enough, indulged in pæans of victory. Renan's response was precisely what might have been expected of him. While he admitted that France had been to blame in declaring war, he pointed out the loss to the world involved in her annihilation, and concluded with a gentle hint to Strauss, that he might profitably bear in mind some precepts of the hero of his best known work: "Have you noticed that, neither in the Beatitudes, nor in the Sermon on the Mount, is there a word giving a place to military virtues among those which gain the Kingdom of God?" Strauss's second letter was even more severe than his first. Its principal point was the stress laid on the fact that Alsace and Lorraine had once been German provinces, and ought to become so once more. Renan met this by a very powerful argument against the annexation of provinces without the consent of their populations,[1] and administered a delicately ironical reproof to his "illustrious master" for having—without permission—published Renan's former letter along with his own two epistles, in a volume the profits of which were devoted to German soldiers wounded in the war. "Heaven preserve me from raising a quibble about literary copyright! Moreover, the act in which you have made me take part is an act of humanity, and if my poor prose has succeeded in procuring a few cigars for those who plundered my little house at Sèvres, I owe you my thanks for having made my conduct conform to what I consider as some of the most authentic precepts of Jesus. But assuredly had you allowed me to publish a production of your pen, never, never should I have dreamt of issuing an edition of it for the benefit of our Hôtel des Invalides."

The Strauss correspondence, along with some of Renan's most weighty contributions to the literature of politics and education, was republished in the volume entitled *La*

[1] The essay entitled "What is a Nation?" on page 61 of this volume, deals with the same theme.

Réforme Intellectuelle et Morale de la France (1871). That France might rise again from her downfall, that even that downfall might ultimately prove to have been her salvation —such was the leading idea running through the various essays of this book, which met with a very hostile reception from Mazzini and other Republican writers, owing to what they considered its retrograde tendency.[1] The fourth volume of the Origins saw the light in 1873. It was entitled *L'Antéchrist*, and continued the history of the early Church from the point at which Renan had left it in *St. Paul.* Nero, Paul, Peter, James, and John all figure in this fascinating part of his history, and a very full treatment is accorded to the remarkable book which we know as the Revelation of St. John, to its probable date and authorship. The remaining volumes of the Origins were *Les Évangiles* (1877), *L'Église Chrétienne* (1879), and *Marc Aurèle* (1882).

Renan had resumed his professorship at the College of France in 1870 (reaching the dignity of Principal three years later); but in April 1871 he left Paris, then under the rule of the Commune, and tried to forget the sickening realities around him in writing the *Dialogues Philosophiques.* The dialogue became a favourite form of expression with Renan in later life; it was admirably adapted to the "double-edged wisdom," the self-abandonment to successive states of mind, which he recommends as being the one thing needful to the modern thinker. In these Philosophical Dialogues, and in the dramas—*Caliban* (1878), *L'Eau de Jouvence*

[1] See *Mazzini's Essays* (Scott Library), p. 299.

(1881), *Le Prêtre de Nemi* (1886), and *L'Abesse de Jouarre* (1886)—one sees his flexibility of idea and utterance to the best advantage. Now in one character he is soaring into the rosy clouds and mists of the ideal, or steeping himself in a passionate mysticism; now he appears as the materialist, the man of positive science and negative criticism. But whatever the character, whatever the turn of thought or expression, one feels that all the time it is Renan who is speaking; Renan who described himself as "a tissue of contradictions, one half of me engaged in devouring the other half, like the fabled beast of Ctesias who ate his own paws without knowing it;" Renan who has words of warning for the man who does not contradict himself at least once a day—"*Malheur à qui ne se contredit pas une fois par jour!*"—Renan who tells one that the only way to be sure of happening on the truth at least once in a lifetime is to be prepared for all contingencies, "to abandon one's self successively to confidence, scepticism, optimism, irony."

At the Spinoza celebration of 1877, Renan delivered the fine address to be found in this volume. With Spinoza he had much in common; especially in respect to the philosophy of practical living, there is considerable resemblance between the views of the seventeenth century sage and the more modern thinker. Claude Bernard, the great physiologist died in 1878, and the French Academy, of which he had been a member, elected Renan to the vacant arm-chair. Renan's address on his reception, as a matter of course, consisted in great part of a eulogy of his predecessor; but he took occasion to restate his views on the world, as it appears from a supernatural and from a scientific point of view. Reality was, he said, far grander than our idea of it; science, while it had destroyed a world of dreams, had given us a world a thousand times more beautiful. With this, one can compare the introduction to his version of the Book of Ecclesiastes published in the same year (1879). "Ring out, church bells," he says in his favourite character of pious sceptic, "for the more you ring, the more shall I allow myself to say that your ringing means nothing definite. Were I afraid of putting you to silence—then, ah then I should become timorous and discreet!"

In the following spring he came to London and delivered the Hibbert lectures of the year, his subject being "Christianity and Rome." A lecture on Marcus Aurelius,[1] delivered at the Royal Institution during this visit, reproduces the salient features of the last volume of the Origins. But perhaps the most interesting event of Renan's later years was a visit which he paid to Tréguier in 1884. The old town itself was very much the same as when he had left it, forty years before, for Paris; but his mother, his sister, and most of the early friends whose portraits he had traced in the *Souvenirs* were dead, and there was a note of pathos in the speech which he delivered in reply to an address of welcome. This visit revived his old love for Brittany, and during the remainder of his life he spent part of each year at Rosmapamon, near Lannion. In the meantime he had been making progress with his last great work, and in 1887

[1] See page 138.

appeared the first volume of the *Histoire du Peuple d'Israël.* Four more volumes followed, two before and two after his death. By the production of this history he brought to a triumphant conclusion the great work of his life—a record and criticism of the origins of Christianity. *Feuilles Detachées* was published in 1892, a book of odds and ends, ranging from after-dinner speeches at the Celtic Club to an "Examination of Philosophic Consciousness," containing his most mature ideas on man and the universe.

The good humour and gaiety of Renan's later writings might well give one the impression, that, in the evening of his life, he enjoyed a well-earned leisure and perfect health. But such was far from being the case. In his latter years his health was very uncertain, although he continued to fill all the obligations which he took upon himself. During 1892 his practical stoicism was manifested in all its grandeur. As early as January he knew that his days were numbered. On October 24th of the previous year he had finished the last volume of the *History of Israel*, and had written at the head of the final chapter, *Finito libro sit laus et gloria Cristo.* But he still had duties to fulfil and tasks to accomplish, and he earnestly hoped for time to do all before his end. In the summer he went as usual to Brittany, but feeling much worse he returned to Paris. There at his post as head of the College of France he passed away on October 2nd. M. Monod tells us that among his last words were, "Let us submit ourselves to the laws of that Nature of which we ourselves are one of the manifestations. The heavens and the earth abide."

To those who had known him he left an ineffaceable memory. There was nothing in his outward appearance to give him charm ; he was small in stature, with an immense head buried between his shoulders, and in his later years especially he was extremely stout. But such external characteristics were forgotten, we are told, when he began to speak. Indeed, his conversational powers were of the highest order. His urbanity was only equalled by his wit, his memory by his imagination; and he was too an admirable story-teller. I cannot but quote from some reminiscences given by Sir Frederick Pollock soon after Renan's death :—

"Most persons who have any character in their faces may be likened, without any violent straining of fancy, to some animal. If I had been commanded to choose a totem-beast for Renan by the law of signatures, I should have chosen a very wise and benevolent toad. But this is said in confidence to people who agree with me in liking toads and not understanding why they are called ugly. When Renan spoke, it was a magical change. One forgot all about his looks, or rather it seemed quite fitting that he should look exactly as he did, and he became manifest as a supreme artist in the rare and difficult art of good talk. Dr. Johnson would have execrated his books if he could have read them, and opened his arms to Renan himself after five minutes' conversation if they could have met. It was the utmost refinement of performance on a fine instrument, and without any stiffness or artificial display."

One who has never heard Renan's voice may form a

conception of his conversation by a study of his prose style. He was the greatest master of modern French prose, which some would interpret as the greatest master of all modern prose. His familiarity with the Bible, with Greek and Latin literature, and with the French classics gave a raiment of antique grace to his modernity. To analyse the magic of his style would be impossible within the present limits, and perhaps in any case fruitless. We may rest contented in the enjoyment of his stately periods, his mordant irony, his ingenuous candour, his daring paradox; and marvel at the subtle interminglement of matter and style, thought and utterance, whereby these two disparate elements seem to lose their dualism and become one.

What I have said of Renan's style might thus serve as an account of his thought. A certain class of critics are vociferous in their demand for a "message"; and to get this "message," they remorselessly boil down the author, who is their victim for the time being, into a solid and somewhat indigestible mass, in which aphorisms are embedded like plums. Renan as a message-bearer would not be a success—he would better indeed fill the part of two or more message-bearers. The faith of his childhood and his ancestors dwelt with him as a sentiment, along with the spirit of agnosticism and free inquiry which had come to him in early manhood. At times he speaks as a mystic overflowing with religious ecstasy; and none has more eloquently interpreted than he the brooding mystery of the infinite, the eternal yearning of humanity towards an ideal, remote by the very law of its being. At times he speaks as a critic—a critic whose last word is that for such fantasies there is no basis of fact within our acquirement; and none has better expressed the contentment of those that see the futility of all desire for the unattainable, and only cherish it æsthetically as a source of poetry, or scientifically as an element of human nature. Joubert's happy description of Montaigne as "*l'homme ondoyant et divers*," could be fittingly used of Montaigne's modern compatriot.

I have already spoken of this seeming inconsistency. It is the most obvious criticism of the man that can be made, and he has made it himself more than once. In his later writings his more festive and ironical turn of mind is chiefly apparent. If this world be not the best of all possible worlds, he would seem to say, it is certainly the most amusing. What more can the philosopher desire? He has only to take his seat in the stalls, and watch the comedy that is being played on the stage before him. "If the world be a bad farce, by gaiety we make it a good one." How much of this is mere surface opinion and how much rooted conviction, I shall not stop to inquire. To Renan might be applied what Lowell has somewhere said of Landor—he was a man of great thoughts rather than a great thinker. To the judicious reader the choice is open. He can take and assimilate the Renan of the essay on Béranger, the Renan who in the preface to his translation of Job tells us that, "Duty with its incalculable philosophical consequences, in imposing itself upon all, resolves all doubts, reconciles all oppositions, and serves as a foundation to rebuild what reason destroys or allows to crumble down." But then, on the other hand, he can betake himself to the other Renan, of the essay on Amiel or the *Souvenirs*, who will point out to him that after all it is quite possible that the virtuous life may be a gigantic fraud, and that the libertine may be the true sage. Renan, in the attitude of a light-hearted spectator of all Time and all Existence, has offended the austerity of such grave and reverend juniors as Mr. Andrew Lang and M. Jules Lemaître. The former, in an article rather lacking in his usual urbanity, describes him as an "elderly and erudite butterfly," while the latter finds that: "As Macbeth murdered sleep, so M. Renan, twenty times, one hundred times, in each of his books has murdered joy, has murdered action, has murdered peace of mind, and the security of the moral life." If such be the case, one can only commiserate M. Lemaître, and advise him to leave this wholesale murderer's works severely alone.

In Renan's discourse on being received into the Academy, he compared the truths of conscience to the revolving gleams of a lighthouse. For a brief space they shine strongly upon us; then they are gone, and we begin to wonder whether we really saw them after all. Perhaps it was so with himself. He had his vision of Deity, not revealed in Nature, which he saw to be immoral, indifferent to good and evil, nor by intelligence ("were man nothing more than intelligent he would be an atheist"); but unveiled in the divine instincts of duty, devotion, and sacrifice, all of which things are without God inexplicable. And even if the "Eternal Verities" were obscured at times, there was always the world to interest him. In the *Child's Garden of Verses* is a couplet which holds Renan's optimism in a nut-shell—

> "The world is so full of a number of things,
> I'm sure we should all be as happy as kings."

It was this interested outlook on the world—and the world of course included himself—that was his safeguard against the pessimism which generally dogs the disillusioned idealist. He himself attributed his good-humoured tolerance of the world and its absurdities to his Catholic education. The emancipated Catholic, he tells us, is fortunate enough "to behold the universe in its infinite splendour, Nature in her high and generous majesty." But note how different is the fate of the most emancipated Protestant; he "retains a touch of sadness, a depth of intellectual austerity analogous to Slavonic pessimism."[1] In writing this Renan might well seem to be criticising a man with whom, despite essential differences, he had much in common. Like Renan, Matthew Arnold was in arms against the hosts of Philistia; like Renan, he cast off formal dogma, but retained an instinctive love and veneration for the religion whose spirit still lived within him. But none the less there remains the fundamental fact, that, while Arnold is stricken with something that at times seems almost blank despair, Renan is in excellent spirits. "Let us," he says, "leave the fortunes of this planet to be accomplished without

[1] See page 196.

troubling ourselves with regard to their conclusion. Our outcries will make no difference, our ill-humour would be out of place. It is quite possible that the earth may be missing her destiny, as probably worlds innumerable have missed theirs. . . But the universe knows not discouragement; each check leaves it young, alert, full of illusions" (*Le Prêtre de Nemi*).

The cheerful resignation of such a passage seems to have an irritant effect upon certain persons, who delight to show their own sincerity by accusing others of the lack of it. A malevolent punster once said of Renan that he was neither earnest nor a Joseph. Whatever the wit of this remark, it is certainly wanting in truth. As for the latter part of the gibe it is nonsensical: Renan was personally as virtuous as though he had signed the Thirty-nine Articles, or subscribed to every tenet of the Church of his fathers. In this respect he followed the example of Spinoza—that is to say, he lived the life of a saint, deeming it inadvisable to shock the minds of the orthodox in more than one way at a time. Nor can the quality of earnest sincerity be denied him. His very inconsistencies can be regarded as but the outward manifestations of a great consistency—a consistency in affirming nothing, in denying nothing, in hoping all. With Pilate he asked, "What is truth?" but he was willing to stay for an answer; he might "count it a bondage to fix a belief," but *Veritatem dilexi* was his chosen epitaph.

WILLIAM G. HUTCHISON.

LONDON, *September* 1896.

Note.—The Translator wishes to acknowledge gratefully the suggestions and criticisms given to him by Mr. Bernard Bosanquet, LL.D., Mr. Joseph Brewis, and Mr. Henry Hooton.

THE POETRY OF THE CELTIC RACES.

EVERY one who travels through the Armorican peninsula experiences a change of the most abrupt description, as soon as he leaves behind the district most closely bordering upon the continent, in which the cheerful but commonplace type of face of Normandy and Maine is continually in evidence, and passes into the true Brittany, that which merits its name by language and race. A cold wind arises full of a vague sadness, and carries the soul to other thoughts; the tree-tops are bare and twisted; the heath with its monotony of tint stretches away into the distance; at every step the granite protrudes from a soil too scanty to cover it; a sea that is almost always sombre girdles the horizon with eternal moaning. The same contrast is manifest in the people: to Norman vulgarity, to a plump and prosperous population, happy to live, full of its own interests, egoistical as are all those who make a habit of enjoyment, succeeds a timid and reserved race living altogether within itself, heavy in appearance but capable of profound feeling, and of an adorable delicacy in its religious instincts. A like change is apparent, I am told, in passing from England into Wales, from the Lowlands of Scotland,

English by language and manners, into the Gaelic Highlands; and too, though with a perceptible difference, when one buries oneself in the districts of Ireland where the race has remained pure from all admixture of alien blood. It seems like entering on the subterranean strata of another world, and one experiences in some measure the impression given us by Dante, when he leads us from one circle of his Inferno to another.

Sufficient attention is not given to the peculiarity of this fact of an ancient race living, until our days and almost under our eyes, its own life in some obscure islands and peninsulas in the West, more and more affected, it is true, by external influences, but still faithful to its own tongue, to its own memories, to its own customs, and to its own genius. Especially is it forgotten that this little people, now concentrated on the very confines of the world, in the midst of rocks and mountains whence its enemies have been powerless to force it, is in possession of a literature which, in the Middle Ages, exercised an immense influence, changed the current of European civilisation, and imposed its poetical motives on nearly the whole of Christendom. Yet it is only necessary to open the authentic monuments of the Gaelic genius to be convinced that the race which created them has had its own original manner of feeling and thinking, that nowhere has the eternal illusion clad itself in more seductive hues, and that in the great chorus of humanity no race equals this for penetrative notes that go to the very heart. Alas! it too is doomed to disappear, this emerald set in the Western seas. Arthur will return no more from his isle of faery, and St. Patrick was right when he said to Ossian, "The heroes that thou weepest are dead; can they be born again?" It is high time to note, before they shall have passed away, the divine tones thus expiring on the horizon before the growing tumult of uniform civilisation. Were criticism to set itself the task of calling back these distant echoes, and of giving a voice to races that are no more, would not that suffice to absolve it from the reproach, unreasonably and too frequently brought against it, of being only negative?

Good works now exist which facilitate the task of him who undertakes the study of these interesting literatures. Wales, above all, is distinguished by scientific and literary activity, not always accompanied, it is true, by a very rigorous critical spirit, but deserving the highest praise. There, researches which would bring honour to the most active centres of learning in Europe are the work of enthusiastic amateurs. A peasant called Owen Jones published in 1801-7, under the name of the *Myvyrian Archaiology of Wales*, the precious collection which is to this day the arsenal of Cymric antiquities. A number of erudite and zealous workers, Aneurin Owen, Thomas Price of Crickhowell, William Rees, and John Jones, following in the footsteps of the Myvyrian peasant, set themselves to finish his work, and to profit from the treasures which he had collected. A woman of distinction, Lady Charlotte Guest, charged herself with the task of acquainting Europe with the collection of the *Mabinogion*,[1] the pearl of Gaelic literature, the completest expression of the Cymric genius. This magnificent work, executed in twelve years with the

[1] *The Mabinogion, from the Llyfr Coch O Hergest and other ancient Welsh Manuscripts, with an English Translation and Notes.* By Lady Charlotte Guest. London and Llandovery, 1837-49. The word *Mabinogi* (in the plural *Mabinogion*) designates a form of romantic narrative peculiar to Wales. The origin and primitive meaning of this word are very uncertain, and Lady Guest's right to apply it to the whole of the narratives which she has published is open to doubt.

luxury that the wealthy English amateur knows how to use in his publications, will one day attest how full of life the consciousness of the Celtic races remained in the present century. Only indeed the sincerest patriotism could inspire a woman to undertake and achieve so vast a literary monument. Scotland and Ireland have in like measure been enriched by a host of studies of their ancient history. Lastly, our own Brittany, though all too rarely studied with the philological and critical rigour now exacted in works of erudition, has furnished Celtic antiquities with her share of worthy research. Does it not suffice to cite M. de la Villemarqué, whose name will be henceforth associated among us with these studies, and whose services are so incontestable, that criticism need have no fear of depreciating him in the eyes of a public which has accepted him with so much warmth and sympathy?

I.

If the excellence of races is to be appreciated by the purity of their blood and the inviolability of their national character, it must needs be admitted that none can vie in nobility with the still surviving remains of the Celtic race.[1] Never has a human family lived more apart from the world, and been purer from all alien admixture. Confined by conquest within forgotten islands and peninsulas, it has reared an impassable barrier against external influences; it

[1] To avoid all misunderstanding, I ought to point out that by the word *Celtic* I designate here, not the whole of the great race which, at a remote epoch, formed the population of nearly the whole of Western Europe, but simply the four groups which, in our days, still merit this name, as opposed to the Teutons and to the Neo-Latin peoples. These four groups are: (1) The inhabitants of Wales or Cambria, and the peninsula of Cornwall, bearing even now the ancient name of

has drawn all from itself; it has lived solely on its own capital. From this ensues that powerful individuality, that hatred of the foreigner, which even in our own days has formed the essential feature of the Celtic peoples. Roman civilisation scarcely reached them, and left among them but few traces. The Teutonic invasion drove them back, but did not penetrate them. At the present hour they are still constant in resistance to an invasion dangerous in an altogether different way,—that of modern civilisation, destructive as it is of local variations and national types. Ireland in particular (and herein we perhaps have the secret of her irremediable weakness) is the only country in Europe where the native can produce the titles of his descent, and designate with certainty, even in the darkness of prehistoric ages, the race from which he has sprung.

It is in this secluded life, in this defiance of all that comes from without, that we must search for the explanation of the chief features of the Celtic character. It has all the failings, and all the good qualities, of the solitary man; at once proud and timid, strong in feeling and feeble in action, at home free and unreserved, to the outside world awkward and embarrassed. It distrusts the foreigner, because it sees in him a being more refined than itself, who abuses its simplicity. Indifferent to the admiration of others, it asks only one thing, that it should be left to itself. It is before all else a domestic race, fitted for family

Cymry; (2) the *Bretons bretonnants*, or dwellers in French Brittany speaking Bas-Breton, who represent an emigration of the Cymry from Wales; (3) the Gaels of the North of Scotland speaking Gaelic; (4) the Irish, although a very profound line of demarcation separates Ireland from the rest of the Celtic family. [It is also necessary to point out that Renan in this essay applies the name *Breton* both to the Bretons proper, *i.e.* the inhabitants of Brittany, and to the British members of the Celtic race.—*Translator's Note.*]

life and fireside joys. In no other race has the bond of blood been stronger, or has it created more duties, or attached man to his fellow with so much breadth and depth. Every social institution of the Celtic peoples was in the beginning only an extension of the family. A common tradition attests, to this very day, that nowhere has the trace of this great institution of relationship been better preserved than in Brittany. There is a widely-spread belief in that country, that blood speaks, and that two relatives, unknown one to the other, in any part of the world wheresoever it may be, recognise each other by the secret and mysterious emotion which they feel in each other's presence. Respect for the dead rests on the same principle. Nowhere has reverence for the dead been greater than among the Breton peoples; nowhere have so many memories and prayers clustered about the tomb. This is because life is not for these people a personal adventure, undertaken by each man on his own account, and at his own risks and perils; it is a link in a long chain, a gift received and handed on, a debt paid and a duty done.

It is easily discernible how little fitted were natures so strongly concentrated to furnish one of those brilliant developments, which imposes the momentary ascendency of a people on the world; and that, no doubt, is why the part played externally by the Cymric race has always been a secondary one. Destitute of the means of expansion, alien to all idea of aggression and conquest, little desirous of making its thought prevail outside itself, it has only known how to retire so far as space has permitted, and then, at bay in its last place of retreat, to make an invincible resistance to its enemies. Its very fidelity has been a useless devotion. Stubborn of submission and ever behind the age, it is faithful to its conquerors when its conquerors are no longer faithful to themselves. It was the last to defend its religious independence against Rome—and it has become the staunchest stronghold of Catholicism; it was the last in France to defend its political independence against the king—and it has given to the world the last royalists.

Thus the Celtic race has worn itself out in resistance to its time, and in the defence of desperate causes. It does not seem as though in any epoch it had any aptitude for political life. The spirit of family stifled within it all attempts at more extended organisation. Moreover, it does not appear that the peoples which form it are by themselves susceptible of progress. To them life appears as a fixed condition, which man has no power to alter. Endowed with little initiative, too much inclined to look upon themselves as minors and in tutelage, they are quick to believe in destiny and resign themselves to it. Seeing how little audacious they are against God, one would scarcely believe this race to be the daughter of Japhet.

Thence ensues its sadness. Take the songs of its bards of the sixth century; they weep more defeats than they sing victories. Its history is itself only one long lament; it still recalls its exiles, its flights across the seas. If at times it seems to be cheerful, a tear is not slow to glisten behind its smile; it does not know that strange forgetfulness of human conditions and destinies which is called gaiety. Its songs of joy end as elegies; there is nothing to equal the delicious sadness of its national melodies. One might call them emanations from on high which, falling drop by drop upon the soul, pass through it like memories of another world. Never have men feasted so long upon these solitary delights of the spirit, these poetic memories which simultaneously intercross all the sensations of life, so vague, so deep, so penetrative, that one might die from them, without being able to say whether it was from bitterness or sweetness.

The infinite delicacy of feeling which characterises the Celtic race is closely allied to its need of concentration. Natures that are little capable of expansion are nearly always those that feel most deeply, for the deeper the feeling, the less it tends to express itself. Thence we have that charming shamefastness, that veiled and exquisite sobriety, equally far removed from the sentimental rhetoric too familiar to the Latin races, and the reflective simplicity of Germany, which are so admirably displayed in the ballads published by M. de la Villemarqué. The apparent reserve of the Celtic peoples, often taken for coldness, is due to this inward timidity which makes them believe that a feeling loses half its value if it be expressed; and that the heart ought to have no other spectator than itself.

If it be permitted us to assign sex to nations as to individuals, we should have to say without hesitance that the Celtic race, especially with regard to its Cymric or Breton branch, is an essentially feminine race. No human family, I believe, has carried so much mystery into love. No other has conceived with more delicacy the ideal of woman, or been more fully dominated by it. It is a sort of intoxication, a madness, a vertigo. Read the strange *Mabinogi of Peredur*, or its French imitation *Parceval le Gallois;* its pages are, as it were, dewy with feminine sentiment. Woman appears therein as a kind of vague vision, an intermediary between man and the supernatural world. I am acquainted with no literature that offers anything analogous to this. Compare Guinevere or Iseult with those Scandinavian furies Gudrun and Chrimhilde, and you will avow that woman such as chivalry conceived her, an ideal of sweetness and loveliness set up as the supreme end of life, is a creation neither classical, nor Christian, nor Teutonic, but in reality Celtic.

Imaginative power is nearly always proportionate to concentration of feeling, and lack of the external development of life. The limited nature of Greek and Italian imagination is due to the easy expansiveness of the peoples of the South, with whom the soul, wholly spread abroad, reflects but little within itself. Compared with the classical imagination, the Celtic imagination is indeed the infinite contrasted with the finite. In the fine *Mabinogi* of the *Dream of Maxen Wledig*, the Emperor Maximus beholds in a dream a young maiden so beautiful, that on waking he declares he cannot live without her. For several years his envoys scour the world in search of her; at last she is discovered in Brittany. So is it with the Celtic race; it has worn itself out in taking dreams for realities, and in pursuing its splendid visions. The essential element in the Celt's poetic life is the *adventure*—that is to say, the pursuit of the unknown, an endless quest after an object ever flying from desire. It was of this that St. Brandan dreamed, that Peredur sought with his mystic chivalry, that Knight Owen asked of his subterranean journeyings. This race desires the infinite, it thirsts for it, and pursues it at all costs, beyond the tomb, beyond hell itself. The characteristic failing of the Breton peoples, the tendency to drunkenness—a failing which, according to the traditions of the sixth century, was the cause of their disasters—is due to this invincible need of illusion. Do not say that it is an appetite for gross enjoyment; never has there been a people more sober and more alien to all sensuality. No, the Bretons sought in mead what Owen, St. Brandan, and Peredur sought in their own way,—the vision of the invisible world. To this day in Ireland drunkenness forms a part of all Saint's Day festivals—that is to say, the festivals which best have retained their national and popular aspect.

Thence arises the profound sense of the future and of the eternal destinies of his race, which has ever borne up the Cymry, and kept him young still beside his conquerors who have grown old. Thence that dogma of the resurrection of the heroes, which appears to have been one of those that Christianity found most difficulty in rooting out. Thence *Celtic Messianism*, that belief in a future avenger who shall restore Cambria, and deliver her out of the hands of her oppressors, like the mysterious Leminok promised by Merlin, the Lez-Breiz of the Armoricans, the Arthur of the Welsh.[1] The hand that arose from the mere, when the sword of Arthur fell therein, that seized it, and brandished it thrice, is the hope of the Celtic races. It is thus that little peoples dowered with imagination revenge themselves on their conquerors. Feeling themselves to be strong inwardly and weak outwardly, they protest, they exult; and such a strife unloosing their might, renders them capable of miracles. Nearly all great appeals to the supernatural are due to peoples hoping against all hope. Who shall say what in our own times has fermented in the bosom of the most stubborn, the most powerless of nationalities,—Poland? Israel in humiliation dreamed of the spiritual conquest of the world, and the dream has come to pass.

II.

At a first glance the literature of Wales is divided into three perfectly distinct branches: the bardic or lyric, which

[1] M. Augustin Thierry has finely remarked that the renown attaching to Welsh prophecies in the Middle Ages was due to their steadfastness in affirming the future of their race. (*Histoire de la Conquête d'Angleterre.*)

shines forth in splendour in the sixth century by the works of Taliessin, of Aneurin, and of Liwarc'h Hên, and continues through an uninterrupted series of imitations up to modern times; the *Mabinogion*, or literature of romance, fixed towards the twelfth century, but linking themselves in the groundwork of their ideas with the remotest ages of the Celtic genius; finally, an ecclesiastical and legendary literature, impressed with a distinct stamp of its own. These three literatures seem to have existed side by side, almost without knowledge of one another. The bards, proud of their solemn rhetoric, held in disdain the popular tales, the form of which they considered careless; on the other hand, both bards and romancers appear to have had few relations with the clergy; and one at times might be tempted to suppose that they ignored the existence of Christianity. To our thinking it is in the *Mabinogion* that the true expression of the Celtic genius is to be sought; and it is surprising that so curious a literature, the source of nearly all the romantic creations of Europe, should have remained unknown until our own days. The cause is doubtless to be ascribed to the dispersed state of the Welsh manuscripts, pursued till last century by the English, as seditious books compromising those who possessed them. Often too they fell into the hands of ignorant owners, whose caprice or ill-will sufficed to keep them from critical research.

The *Mabinogion* have been preserved for us in two principal documents—one of the thirteenth century from the library of Hengurt, belonging to the Vaughan family; the other dating from the fourteenth century, known under the name of the *Red Book of Hergest*, and now in Jesus College, Oxford. No doubt it was some such collection that charmed the weary hours of the hapless Leolin in the

Tower of London, and was burned after his condemnation, with the other Welsh books which had been the companions of his captivity. Lady Charlotte Guest has based her edition on the Oxford manuscript; it cannot be sufficiently regretted that paltry considerations have caused her to be refused the use of the earlier manuscript, of which the later appears to be only a copy. Regrets are redoubled when one knows that several Welsh texts, which were seen and copied fifty years ago, have now disappeared. It is in the presence of facts such as these that one comes to believe that revolutions—in general so destructive of the works of the past—are favourable to the preservation of literary monuments, by compelling their concentration in great centres, where their existence, as well as their publicity, is assured.

The general tone of the *Mabinogion* is rather romantic than epic. Life is treated naïvely and not too emphatically. The hero's individuality is limitless. We have free and noble natures acting in all their spontaneity. Each man appears as a kind of demi-god characterised by a supernatural gift. This gift is nearly always connected with some miraculous object, which in some measure is the personal seal of him who possesses it. The inferior classes, which this people of heroes necessarily supposes beneath it, scarcely show themselves, except in the exercise of some trade, for practising which they are held in high esteem. The somewhat complicated products of human industry are regarded as living beings, and in their manner endowed with magical properties. A multiplicity of celebrated objects have proper names, such as the drinking-cup, the lance, the sword, and the shield of Arthur; the chess-board of Gwendolen, on which the black pieces played of their own accord against the white; the horn of Bran Galed, where one found whatever liquor one desired; the chariot of Morgan, which directed itself to the place to which one wished to go; the pot of Tyrnog, which would not cook when meat for a coward was put into it; the grindstone of Tudwal, which would only sharpen brave men's swords; the coat of Padarn, which none save a noble could don; and the mantle of Tegan, which no woman could put upon herself were she not above reproach.[1] The animal is conceived in a still more individual way; it has a proper name, personal qualities, and a rôle which it develops at its own will and with full consciousness. The same hero appears as at once man and animal, without it being possible to trace the line of demarcation between the two natures.

The tale of *Kilhwch and Olwen*, the most extraordinary of the *Mabinogion*, deals with Arthur's struggle against the wild-boar king Twrch Trwyth, who with his seven cubs holds in check all the heroes of the Round Table. The adventures of the three hundred ravens of Kerverhenn similarly form the subject of the *Dream of Rhonabwy*. The idea of moral merit and demerit is almost wholly absent from all these compositions. There are wicked beings who insult ladies, who tyrannise over their neighbours, who only find pleasure in evil because such is their nature; but it does not appear that they incur wrath on that account. Arthur's knights pursue them, not as criminals but as mischievous fellows. All other beings are perfectly good and just, but more or less richly gifted. This is the dream of an amiable and gentle race which looks upon evil as being the work of destiny, and not a product of the human conscience. All nature is enchanted, and fruitful as imagination itself in indefinitely varied creations.

[1] Here may be recognised the origin of trial by *court mantle*, one of the most interesting episodes in *Lancelot of the Lake*.

Christianity rarely discloses itself; although at times its proximity can be felt, it alters in no respect the purely natural surroundings in which everything takes place. A bishop figures at table beside Arthur, but his function is strictly limited to blessing the dishes. The Irish saints, who at one time present themselves to give their benediction to Arthur and receive favours at his hands, are portrayed as a race of men vaguely known and difficult to understand. No mediæval literature held itself further removed from all monastic influence. We evidently must suppose that the Welsh bards and story-tellers lived in a state of great isolation from the clergy, and had their culture and traditions quite apart.

The charm of the *Mabinogion* principally resides in the amiable serenity of the Celtic mind, neither sad nor gay, ever in suspense between a smile and a tear. We have in them the simple recital of a child, unwitting of any distinction between the noble and the common; there is something of that softly animated world, of that calm and tranquil ideal to which Ariosto's stanzas transport us. The chatter of the later mediæval French and German imitators can give no idea of this charming manner of narration. The skilful Chrétien de Troyes[1] himself remains in this respect far below the Welsh story-tellers, and as for Wolfram of Eschenbach,[2] it must be avowed that the joy of the first discovery has carried German critics too far in the exaggeration of his merits. He loses himself in interminable descriptions, and almost completely ignores the art of his recital.

What strikes one at a first glance in the imaginative compositions of the Celtic races, above all when they are contrasted with those of the Teutonic races, is the extreme

[1] See Note I. [2] See Note II.

mildness of manners pervading them. There are none of those frightful vengeances which fill the *Edda* and the *Niebelungen*. Compare the Teutonic with the Gaelic hero, —Beowulf with Peredur, for example. What a difference there is! In the one all the horror of disgusting and blood-embrued barbarism, the drunkenness of carnage, the disinterested taste, if I may say so, for destruction and death; in the other a profound sense of justice, a great height of personal pride it is true, but also a great capacity for devotion, an exquisite loyalty. The tyrannical man, the monster, the *Black Man*, find a place here like the Lestrigons and the Cyclops of Homer only to inspire horror by contrast with softer manners; they are almost what the wicked man is in the naïve imagination of a child brought up by a mother in the ideas of a gentle and pious morality. The primitive man of Teutonism is revolting by his purposeless brutality, by a love of evil that only gives him skill and strength in the service of hatred and injury. The Cymric hero on the other hand, even in his wildest flights, seems possessed by habits of kindness and a warm sympathy with the weak. Sympathy indeed is one of the deepest feelings among the Celtic peoples. Even Judas is not denied a share of their pity. St. Brandan found him upon a rock in the midst of the Polar seas; once a week he passes a day there to refresh himself from the fires of hell. A cloak that he had given to a beggar is hung before him, and tempers his sufferings.

If Wales has a right to be proud of her *Mabinogion*, she has not less to felicitate herself in having found a translator truly worthy of interpreting them. For the proper understanding of these original beauties there was needed a delicate appreciation of Welsh narration, and an intelligence of the naïve order, qualities of which an erudite translator would with difficulty have been capable. To render these gracious imaginings of a people so eminently dowered with feminine tact, the pen of a woman was necessary. Simple, animated, without effort and without vulgarity, Lady Guest's translation is the faithful mirror of the original Cymric. Even supposing that, as regards philology, the labours of this noble Welsh lady be destined to receive improvement, that does not prevent her book from for ever remaining a work of erudition and highly distinguished taste.[1]

The *Mabinogion*, or at least the writings which Lady Guest thought she ought to include under this common name, divide themselves into two perfectly distinct classes—some connected exclusively with the two peninsulas of Wales and Cornwall, and relating to the heroic personality of Arthur; the others alien to Arthur, having for their scene not only the parts of England that have remained Cymric, but the whole of Great Britain, and leading us back by the persons and traditions mentioned in them to the later years of the Roman occupation. The second class, of greater antiquity than the first, at least on the ground of subject, is also distinguished by a much more mythological character, a bolder use of the miraculous, an enigmatical form, a style full of alliteration and plays upon words. Of this number are the tales of *Pwyll*, of *Branwen*, of *Manawyddan*, of *Math the son of Mathonwy*, the *Dream of the Emperor Maximus*, the story of *Llud and Llewelys*, and the legend of Taliessin. To the Arthurian cycle belong the narratives of *Owen*, of *Geraint*, of *Peredur*, of *Kilhwch and Olwen*, and the *Dream of Rhonabwy*. It is also to be remarked that

[1] M. de la Villemarqué published in 1842 under the title of *Contes populaires des anciens Bretons*, a French translation of the narratives that Lady Guest had already presented in English at that time.

the two last-named narratives have a particularly antique character. In them Arthur dwells in Cornwall, and not as in the others at Caerleon on the Usk. In them he appears with an individual character, hunting and taking a personal part in warfare, while in the more modern tales he is only an emperor all-powerful and impassive, a truly sluggard hero, around whom a pleiad of active heroes groups itself. The *Mabinogi* of *Kilhwch and Olwen*, by its entirely primitive aspect, by the part played in it by the wild-boar in conformity to the spirit of Celtic mythology, by the wholly supernatural and magical character of the narration, by innumerable allusions the sense of which escapes us, forms a cycle by itself. It represents for us the Cymric conception in all its purity, before it had been modified by the introduction of any foreign element. Without attempting here to analyse this curious poem, I should like by some extracts to make its antique aspect and high originality apparent.

Kilhwch, son of Kilydd, prince of Kelyddon, having heard some one mention the name of Olwen, daughter of Yspaddaden Penkawr, falls violently in love, without having ever seen her. He goes to find Arthur, that he may ask for his aid in the difficult undertaking which he meditates; in point of fact, he does not know in what country the fair one of his affection dwells. Yspaddaden is besides a frightful tyrant who suffers no man to go from his castle alive, and whose death is linked by destiny to the marriage of his daughter.[1] Arthur grants Kilhwch some of his most valiant comrades in arms to assist him in this enterprise. After wonderful adventures the knights arrive at the castle

[1] The idea of making the death of the father the condition of possession of the daughter is to be found in several romances of the Breton cycle, in *Lancelot* for example.

of Yspaddaden, and succeed in seeing the young maiden of Kilhwch's dream. Only after three days of persistent struggle do they manage to obtain a response from Olwen's father, who attaches his daughter's hand to conditions apparently impossible of realisation. The performance of these trials makes a long chain of adventures, the framework of a veritable romantic epic which has come to us in a very fragmentary form. Of the thirty-eight adventures imposed on Kilhwch the manuscript used by Lady Guest only relates seven or eight. I choose at random one of these narratives, which appears to me fitted to give an idea of the whole composition. It deals with the finding of Mabon the son of Modron, who was carried away from his mother three days after his birth, and whose deliverance is one of the labours exacted of Kilhwch.

"His followers said unto Arthur, 'Lord, go thou home; thou canst not proceed with thy host in quest of such small adventures as these.' Then said Arthur, 'It were well for thee, Gwrhyr Gwalstawd Ieithoedd, to go upon this quest, for thou knowest all languages, and art familiar with those of the birds and the beasts. Thou, Eidoel, oughtest likewise to go with my men in search of thy cousin. And as for you, Kai and Bedwyr, I have hope of whatever adventure ye are in quest of, that ye will achieve it. Achieve ye this adventure for me.'"

They went forward until they came to the Ousel of Cilgwri. And Gwrhyr adjured her for the sake of Heaven, saying, "Tell me if thou knowest aught of Mabon the son of Modron, who was taken when three nights old from between his mother and the wall." And the Ousel answered, "When I first came here there was a smith's anvil in this place, and I was then a young bird; and from that time no work has been done upon it, save the pecking of my beak every evening, and now there is not so much as the size of a nut remaining thereof; yet all the vengeance of Heaven be upon me, if during all that time I have ever heard of the man for whom you enquire. Nevertheless I will do that which is right, and that which it is fitting I should do for an embassy from Arthur. There is a race of animals who were formed before me, and I will be your guide to them."

So they proceeded to the place where was the Stag of Redynvre. "Stag of Redynvre, behold we are come to thee, an embassy from Arthur, for we have not heard of any animal older than thou. Say, knowest thou aught of Mabon the son of Modron, who was taken from his mother when three nights old?" The Stag said, "When first I came hither there was a plain all around me, without any trees save one oak sapling, which grew up to be an oak with an hundred branches. And that oak has since perished, so that now nothing remains of it but the withered stump; and from that day to this I have been here, yet have I never heard of the man for whom you enquire. Nevertheless, being an embassy from Arthur, I will be your guide to the place where there is an animal which was formed before I was."

So they proceeded to the place where was the Owl of Cwm Cawlwyd. "Owl of Cwm Cawlwyd, here is an embassy from Arthur; knowest thou aught of Mabon the son of Modron, who was taken after three nights from his mother?" "If I knew I would tell you. When first I came hither, the wide valley you see was a wooded glen. And a race of men came and rooted it up. And there grew there a second wood; and this wood is the third. My wings, are they not withered stumps? Yet all this time, even until to-day, I have never heard of the man for whom you enquire. Nevertheless I will be the guide of Arthur's embassy until you come to the place where is the oldest animal in the world, and the one that has travelled most, the Eagle of Gwern Abwy."

Gwrhyr said, "Eagle of Gwern Abwy, we have come to thee an embassy from Arthur, to ask thee if thou knowest aught of Mabon the son of Modron, who was taken from his mother when he was three nights old." The Eagle said, "I have been here for a great space of time, and when I first came hither there was a rock here, from the top of which I pecked at the stars every evening; and now it is not so much as a span high. From that day to this I have been here, and I have never heard of the man for whom you enquire, except once when I went in search of food as far as Llyn Llyw. And when I came there, I struck my talons into a salmon, thinking he would serve me as food for a long time. But he drew me into the deep, and I was scarcely able to escape from him. After that I went with my whole kindred to attack him, and to try to destroy him, but he sent messengers, and made peace with me; and came and besought me to take fifty fish spears out of his back. Unless he know something of him whom you seek, I cannot tell who may. However, I will guide you to the place where he is."

So they went thither; and the Eagle said, "Salmon of Llyn Llyw, I have come to thee with an embassy from Arthur, to ask thee if thou knowest aught concerning Mabon the son of Modron, who was taken away at three nights old from his mother." "As much as I know I will tell thee. With every tide I go along the river upwards, until I come near to the walls of Gloucester, and there have I found such wrong as I never found elsewhere; and to the end that ye may give credence thereto, let one of you go thither upon each of my two shoulders." So Kai and Gwrhyr Gwalstawd Ieithoedd went upon the shoulders of the salmon, and they proceeded until they came unto the wall of the prison, and they heard a great wailing and lamenting from the dungeon. Said Gwrhyr, "Who is it that laments in this house of stone?" "Alas there is reason enough for whoever is here to lament. It is Mabon the son of Modron who is here imprisoned; and no imprisonment was ever so grievous as mine, neither that of Lludd Llaw Ereint, nor that of Greid the son of Eri." "Hast thou hope of being released for gold or for silver, or for any gifts of wealth, or through battle and fighting?" "By fighting will whatever I may gain be obtained."

We shall not follow the Cymric hero through trials the result of which can be foreseen. What, above all else, is striking in these strange legends is the part played by animals, transformed by the Welsh imagination into intelligent beings. No race conversed so intimately as did the Celtic race with the lower creation, and accorded it so large a share of moral life.[1] The close association of man and animal, the fictions so dear to mediæval poetry of the *Knight of the Lion*, the *Knight of the Falcon*, the *Knight of the Swan*, the vows consecrated by the presence of birds of noble repute, are equally Breton imaginings. Ecclesiastical literature itself presents analogous features; gentleness towards animals informs all the legends of the saints of Brittany and Ireland. One day St. Kevin fell asleep, while he was praying at his window with outstretched arms; and a swallow perceiving the open hand of the venerable monk, considered it an excellent place wherein to make her nest. The saint on awaking saw the mother

[1] See especially the narratives of Nennius, and of Giraldus Cambrensis. In them animals have at least as important a part as men.

sitting upon her eggs, and, loth to disturb her, waited for the little ones to be hatched before he arose from his knees.

This touching sympathy was derived from the singular vivacity with which the Celtic races have inspired their feeling for nature. Their mythology is nothing more than a transparent naturalism, not that anthropomorphic naturalism of Greece and India, in which the forces of the universe, viewed as living beings and endowed with consciousness, tend more and more to detach themselves from physical phenomena, and to become moral beings; but in some measure a realistic naturalism, the love of nature for herself, the vivid impression of her magic, accompanied by the sorrowful feeling that man knows, when, face to face with her, he believes that he hears her commune with him concerning his origin and his destiny. The legend of Merlin mirrors this feeling. Seduced by a fairy of the woods, he flies with her and becomes a savage. Arthur's messengers come upon him as he is singing by the side of a fountain; he is led back again to court; but the charm carries him away. He returns to his forests, and this time for ever. Under a thicket of hawthorn Vivien has built him a magical prison. There he prophesies the future of the Celtic races; he speaks of a maiden of the woods, now visible and now unseen, who holds him captive by her spells. Several Arthurian legends are impressed with the same character. Arthur himself in popular belief became, as it were, a woodland spirit. "The foresters on their nightly round by the light of the moon,"[1] says Gervais of Tilbury, "often hear a great sound as of horns, and meet bands of huntsmen; when they are asked whence they come, these huntsmen

[1] See Note III.

make reply that they are of King Arthur's following."[1] Even the French imitators of the Breton romances keep an impression—although a rather insipid one—of the attraction exercised by nature on the Celtic imagination. Elaine, the heroine of Lancelot, the ideal of Breton perfection, passes her life with her companions in a garden, in the midst of flowers which she tends. Every flower culled by her hands is at the instant restored to life; and the worshippers of her memory are under an obligation, when they cut a flower, to sow another in its place.

The worship of forest, and fountain, and stone is to be explained by this primitive naturalism, which all the Councils of the Church held in Brittany united to proscribe. The stone, in truth, seems the natural symbol of the Celtic races. It is an immutable witness that has no death. The animal, the plant, above all the human figure, only express the divine life under a determinate form; the stone on the contrary, adapted to receive all forms, has been the fetish of peoples in their childhood. Pausanias saw, still standing erect, the thirty square stones of Pharæ, each bearing the name of a divinity. The *men-hir* to be met with over the whole surface of the ancient world, what is it but the monument of primitive humanity, a living witness of its faith in Heaven?[2]

[1] This manner of explaining all the unknown noises of the wood by *Arthur's Hunting* is still to be found in several districts. To understand properly the cult of nature, and, if I may say so, of landscape among the Celts, see Gildas and Nennius, pp. 131, 136, 137, etc. (Edit. San Marte, Berlin, 1844).

[2] It is, however, doubtful whether the monuments known in France as *Celtic* (*men-hir*, *dol-men*, etc.) are the work of the Celts. With M. Worsaae and the Copenhagen archæologists, I am inclined to think that these monuments belong to a more ancient humanity. Never, in fact, has any branch of the Indo-European race built in this fashion. (See two articles by M. Mérimée in *L'Athenæum français*, Sept. 11th, 1852, and April 25th, 1853.)

It has frequently been observed that the majority of popular beliefs still extant in our different provinces are of Celtic origin. A not less remarkable fact is the strong tinge of naturalism dominant in these beliefs. Nay more, every time that the old Celtic spirit appears in our history, there is to be seen, re-born with it, faith in nature and her magic influences. One of the most characteristic of these manifestations seems to me to be that of Joan of Arc. That indomitable hope, that tenacity in the affirmation of the future, that belief that the salvation of the kingdom will come from a woman,—all those features, far removed as they are from the taste of antiquity, and from Teutonic taste, are in many respects Celtic. The memory of the ancient cult perpetuated itself at Domremy, as in so many other places, under the form of popular superstition. The cottage of the family of Arc was shaded by a beech tree, famed in the country and reputed to be the abode of fairies. In her childhood Joan used to go and hang upon its branches garlands of leaves and flowers, which, so it was said, disappeared during the night. The terms of her accusation speak with horror of this innocent custom, as of a crime against the faith; and indeed they were not altogether deceived, those unpitying theologians who judged the holy maid. Although she knew it not, she was more Celtic than Christian. She has been foretold by Merlin; she knows of neither Pope nor Church,—she only believes the voice that speaks in her own heart. This voice she hears in the fields, in the sough of the wind among the trees, when measured and distant sounds fall upon her ears. During her trial, worn out with questions and scholastic subtleties, she is asked whether she still hears her voices. "Take me to the woods," she says, "and I shall hear them clearly." Her legend is tinged with the same colours;

nature loved her, the wolves never touched the sheep of her flock. When she was a little girl, the birds used to come and eat bread from her lap as though they were tame.[1]

III.

The *Mabinogion* do not recommend themselves to our study, only as a manifestation of the romantic genius of the Breton races. It was through them that the Welsh imagination exercised its influence upon the Continent, that it transformed, in the twelfth century, the poetic art of Europe, and realised this miracle,—that the creations of a half-conquered race have become the universal feast of imagination for mankind.

Few heroes owe less to reality than Arthur. Neither Gildas nor Aneurin, his contemporaries, speak of him; Bede did not even know his name; Taliessin and Liwarc'h Hên gave him only a secondary place. In Nennius, on the other hand, who lived about 850, the legend has fully unfolded. Arthur is already the exterminator of the Saxons; he has never experienced defeat; he is the suzerain of an army of kings. Finally, in Geoffrey of Monmouth, the epic creation culminates. Arthur reigns over the whole earth; he conquers Ireland, Norway, Gascony, and France. At Caerleon he holds a tournament at which all the

[1] Since the first publication of these views, on which I should not like more emphasis to be put than what belongs to a passing impression, similar considerations have been developed, in terms that appear a little too positive, by M. H. Martin (*History of France*, vol. vi., 1856). The objections raised to it are, for the most part, due to the fact that very few people are capable of delicately appreciating questions of this kind, relative to the genius of races. It frequently happens that the resurrection of an old national genius takes place under a very different form from that which one would have expected, and by means of individuals who have no idea of the ethnographical part which they play.

monarchs of the world are present; there he puts upon his head thirty crowns, and exacts recognition as the sovereign lord of the universe. So incredible is it that a petty king of the sixth century, scarcely remarked by his contemporaries, should have taken in posterity such colossal proportions, that several critics have supposed that the legendary Arthur and the obscure chieftain who bore that name have nothing in common, the one with the other, and that the son of Uther Pendragon is a wholly ideal hero, a survivor of the old Cymric mythology. As a matter of fact, in the symbols of Neo-Druidism—that is to say, of that secret doctrine, the outcome of Druidism, which prolonged its existence even to the Middle Ages under the form of Freemasonry—we again find Arthur transformed into a divine personage, and playing a purely mythological part. It must at least be allowed that, if behind the fable some reality lies hidden, history offers us no means of attaining it. It cannot be doubted that the discovery of Arthur's tomb in the Isle of Avalon in 1189 was an invention of Norman policy, just as in 1283, the very year in which Edward I. was engaged in crushing out the last vestiges of Welsh independence, Arthur's crown was very conveniently found, and forthwith united to the other crown jewels of England.

We naturally expect Arthur, now become the representative of Welsh nationality, to sustain in the *Mabinogion* a character analogous to this rôle, and therein, as in Nennius, to serve the hatred of the vanquished against the Saxons. But such is not the case. Arthur, in the *Mabinogion*, exhibits no characteristics of patriotic resistance; his part is limited to uniting heroes around him, to maintaining the retainers of his palace, and to enforcing the laws of his order of chivalry. He is too strong for any one to dream of attacking him. He is the Charlemagne of the Carlovingian romances, the Agamemnon of Homer,—one of those neutral personalities that serve but to give unity to the poem. The idea of warfare against the alien, hatred towards the Saxon, does not appear in a single instance. The heroes of the *Mabinogion* have no fatherland; each fights to show his personal excellence, and satisfy his taste for adventure, but not to defend a national cause. Britain is the universe; no one suspects that beyond the Cymry there may be other nations and other races.

It was by this ideal and representative character that the Arthurian legend had such an astonishing prestige throughout the whole world. Had Arthur been only a provincial hero, the more or less happy defender of a little country, all peoples would not have adopted him, any more than they have adopted the Marco of the Serbs,[1] or the Robin Hood of the Saxons. The Arthur who has charmed the world is the head of an order of equality, in which all sit at the same table, in which a man's worth depends upon his valour and his natural gifts. What mattered to the world the fate of an unknown peninsula, and the strife waged on its behalf? What enchanted it was the ideal court presided over by Gwenhwyvar (Guinevere), where around the monarchical unity the flower of heroes was gathered together, where ladies, as chaste as they were beautiful, loved according to the laws of chivalry, and where the time was passed in listening to stories, and learning civility and beautiful manners.

This is the secret of the magic of that Round Table, about which the Middle Ages grouped all their ideas of heroism, of beauty, of modesty, and of love. We need not stop to inquire whether the ideal of a gentle and polished society in the midst of the barbarian world is, in all its features, a purely Breton creation, whether the spirit of the courts of

[1] See Note IV.

the Continent has not in some measure furnished the model, and whether the *Mabinogion* themselves have not felt the reaction of the French imitations;[1] it suffices for us that the new order of sentiments which we have just indicated was, throughout the whole of the Middle Ages, persistently attached to the groundwork of the Cymric romances. Such an association could not be fortuitous; if the imitations are all so glaring in colour, it is evidently because in the original this same colour is to be found united to particularly strong character. How otherwise shall we explain why a forgotten tribe on the very confines of the world should have imposed its heroes upon Europe, and, in the domain of imagination, accomplished one of the most singular revolutions known to the historian of letters?

If, in fact, one compares European literature before the introduction of the Cymric romances, with what it became when the *trouvères* set themselves to draw from Breton sources, one recognises readily that with the Breton narratives a new element entered into the poetic conception of the Christian peoples, and modified it profoundly. The Carlovingian poem, both by its structure and by the means which it employs, does not depart from classical ideas. The motives of man's action are the same as in the Greek epic. The essentially romantic element, the life of forests and mysterious adventure, the feeling for nature, and that impulse of imagination which makes the Breton warrior unceasingly pursue the unknown;—nothing of all this is as yet to be observed. Roland differs from the heroes of

[1] The surviving version of the *Mabinogion* has a later date than these imitations, and the Red Book includes several tales borrowed from the French *trouvères*. But it is out of the question to maintain that the really Welsh narratives have been borrowed in a like manner, since among them are some unknown to the *trouvères*, which could only possess interest for Breton countries.

Homer only by his armour; in heart he is the brother of Ajax or Achilles. Perceval, on the contrary, belongs to another world, separated by a great gulf from that in which the heroes of antiquity live and act.

It was above all by the creation of woman's character, by introducing into mediæval poetry, hitherto hard and austere, the *nuances* of love, that the Breton romances brought about this curious metamorphosis. It was like an electric spark; in a few years European taste was changed. Nearly all the types of womankind known to the Middle Ages, Guinevere, Iseult, Enid, are derived from Arthur's court. In the Carlovingian poems woman is a nonentity without character or individuality; in them love is either brutal, as in the romance of *Ferebras*, or scarcely indicated, as in the *Song of Roland*. In the *Mabinogion*, on the other hand, the principal part always belongs to the women. Chivalrous gallantry, which makes the warrior's happiness to consist in serving a woman and meriting her esteem, the belief that the noblest use of strength is to succour and avenge weakness, results, I know, from a turn of imagination which possessed nearly all European peoples in the twelfth century; but it cannot be doubted that this turn of imagination first found literary expression among the Breton peoples. One of the most surprising features in the *Mabinogion* is the delicacy of the feminine feeling breathed in them; an impropriety or a gross word is never to be met with. It would be necessary to quote at length the two romances of *Peredur* and *Geraint* to demonstrate an innocence such as this; but the naïve simplicity of these charming compositions forbids us to see in this innocence any underlying meaning. The zeal of the knight in the defence of ladies' honour became a satirical euphemism only in the French imitators, who transformed the virginal modesty of the Breton romances into a shameless gallantry —so far indeed that these compositions, chaste as they are in the original, became the scandal of the Middle Ages, provoked censures, and were the occasion of the ideas of immorality which, for religious people, still cluster about the name of *romance*.

Certainly chivalry is too complex a fact for us to be permitted to assign it to any single origin. Let us say however that in the idea of envisaging the esteem of a woman as the highest object of human activity, and setting up love as the supreme principle of morality, there is nothing of the antique spirit, or indeed of the Teutonic. Is it in the *Edda* or in the *Niebelungen* that we shall find the germ of this spirit of pure love, of exalted devotion, which forms the very soul of chivalry? As to following the suggestion of some critics and seeking among the Arabs for the beginnings of this institution, surely of all literary paradoxes ever mooted, this is one of the most singular. The idea of conquering woman in a land where she is bought and sold, of seeking her esteem in a land where she is scarcely considered capable of moral merit! I shall oppose the partizans of this hypothesis with one single fact,—the surprise experienced by the Arabs of Algeria when, by a somewhat unfortunate recollection of mediæval tournaments, the ladies were entrusted with the presentation of prizes at the Beiram races. What to the knight appeared an unparalleled honour seemed to the Arabs a humiliation and almost an insult.

The introduction of the Breton romances into the current of European literature worked a not less profound revolution in the manner of conceiving and employing the marvellous. In the Carlovingian poems the marvellous is timid, and conforms to the Christian faith; the supernatural is produced directly by God or his envoys. Among the Cymry, on the contrary, the principle of the marvel is in nature herself, in her hidden forces, in her inexhaustible fecundity. There is a mysterious swan, a prophetic bird, a suddenly appearing hand, a giant, a black tyrant, a magic mist, a dragon, a cry that causes the hearer to die of terror, an object with extraordinary properties. There is no trace of the monotheistic conception, in which the marvellous is only a miracle, a derogation of eternal laws. Nor are there any of those personifications of the life of nature which form the essential part of the Greek and Indian mythologies. Here we have perfect naturalism, an unlimited faith in the possible, belief in the existence of independent beings bearing within themselves the principle of their strength,—an idea quite opposed to Christianity, which in such beings necessarily sees either angels or fiends. And besides, these strange beings are always presented as being outside the pale of the Church; and when the knight of the Round Table has conquered them, he forces them to go and pay homage to Guinevere, and have themselves baptised.

Now, if in poetry there is a marvellous element that we might accept, surely it is this. Classical mythology, taken in its first simplicity, is too bold, taken as a mere figure of rhetoric, too insipid, to give us satisfaction. As to the marvellous element in Christianity, Boileau is right: no fiction is compatible with such a dogmatism. There remains then the purely naturalistic marvellous, nature interesting herself in action and acting herself, the great mystery of fatality unveiling itself by the secret conspiring of all beings, as in Shakespeare and Ariosto. It would be curious to ascertain how much of the Celt there is in the former of these poets; as for Ariosto he is the Breton poet *par excellence*. All his machinery, all his means of interest, all his fine shades of sentiment, all his types of women, all his adventures, are borrowed from the Breton romances.

Do we now understand the intellectual rôle of that little race which gave to the world Arthur, Guinevere, Lancelot, Perceval, Merlin, St. Brandan, St. Patrick, and almost all the poetical cycles of the Middle Ages? What a striking destiny some nations have, in alone possessing the right to cause the acceptance of their heroes, as though for that were necessary a quite peculiar degree of authority, seriousness, and faith! And it is a strange thing that it is to the Normans, of all peoples the one least sympathetically inclined towards the Bretons, that we owe the renown of the Breton fables. Brilliant and imitative, the Norman everywhere became the pre-eminent representative of the nation on which he had at first imposed himself by force. French in France, English in England, Italian in Italy, Russian at Novgorod, he forgot his own language to speak that of the race which he had conquered, and to become the interpreter of its genius. The deeply suggestive character of the Welsh romances could not fail to impress men so prompt to seize and assimilate the ideas of the foreigner. The first revelation of the Breton fables, the Latin Chronicle of Geoffrey of Monmouth, appeared about the year 1137, under the auspices of Robert of Gloucester, natural son of Henry I. Henry II. acquired a taste for the same narratives, and at his request Robert Wace, in 1155, wrote in French the first history of Arthur, thus opening the path in which walked after him a host of poets or imitators of all nationalities, French, Provençal, Italian, Spanish, English, Scandinavian, Greek, and Georgian. We need not belittle the glory of the first *trouvères* who put into a language, then read and understood from one end of Europe to the other, fictions which, but for them, would have doubtless remained for ever unknown. It is however difficult to attribute to them an inventive faculty, such as would permit them to merit the title of creators. The numerous passages in which one feels that they do not fully understand the original which they imitate, and in which they attempt to give a natural significance to circumstances of which the mythological bearing escaped them, suffice to prove that, as a rule, they were satisfied to make a fairly faithful copy of the work before their eyes.

What part has Armorican Brittany played in the creation or propagation of the legends of the Round Table? It is impossible to say with any degree of precision; and in truth such a question becomes a matter of secondary import, once we form a just idea of the close bonds of fraternity, which did not cease until the twelfth century to unite the two branches of the Breton peoples. That the heroic traditions of Wales long continued to live in the branch of the Cymric family which came and settled in Armorica cannot be doubted when we find Geraint, Urien, and other heroes become saints in Lower Brittany;[1] and above all when we see one of the most essential episodes of the Arthurian cycle, that of the Forest of Brocéliande, placed in the same country. A large number of facts collected by M. de la Villemarqué[2] prove, on the other hand, that these

[1] I shall only cite a single proof; it is a law of Edward the Confessor: "Britones vero Armorici quum venerint in regno isto, suscipi debent et in regno protegi sicut probi cives de corpore regni hujus; exierunt quondam de sanguine Britonum regni hujus."—Wilkins, *Leges Anglo-Saxonicæ*, p. 206.

[2] *Les Romans de la Table-Ronde et les contes des anciens Bretons* (Paris, 1859), pp. 20 *et seq.* In the *Contes populaires des anciens Bretons*, of which the above may be considered as a new edition, the learned author had somewhat exaggerated the influence of French Brittany. In the present article, when first published, I had, on the other hand, depreciated it too much.

same traditions produced a true poetic cycle in Brittany, and even that at certain epochs they must have recrossed the Channel, as though to give new life to the mother country's memories. The fact that Gauthier Calenius, Archdeacon of Oxford, brought back from Brittany to England (about 1125) the very text of the legends which were translated into Latin ten years afterwards by Geoffrey of Monmouth is here decisive. I know that to readers of the *Mabinogion* such an opinion will appear surprising at a first glance. All is Welsh in these fables, the places, the genealogies, the customs; in them Armorica is only represented by Hoel, an important personage no doubt, but one who has not achieved the fame of the other heroes of Arthur's court. Again, if Armorica saw the birth of the Arthurian cycle, how is it that we fail to find there any traces of that brilliant nativity?[1]

These objections, I avow, long barred my way, but I no longer find them insoluble. And first of all there is a class of *Mabinogion*, including those of Owen, Geraint, and Peredur, stories which possess no very precise geographical localisation. In the second place, national written literature being less successfully defended in Brittany than in Wales against the invasion of foreign culture, it may be conceived that the memory of the old epics should be there more obliterated. The literary share of the two countries thus remains sufficiently distinct. The glory of French Brittany is in her popular songs; but it is only in Wales that the genius of the Breton people has succeeded in establishing itself in authentic books and achieved creations.

[1] M. de la Villemarqué makes appeal to the popular songs still extant in Brittany, in which Arthur's deeds are celebrated. In fact, in his *Chants populaires de la Bretagne* two poems are to be found in which that hero's name figures.

IV.

In comparing the Breton cycle as the French *trouvères* knew it, and the same cycle as it is to be found in the text of the *Mabinogion*, one might be tempted to believe that the European imagination, enthralled by these brilliant fables, added to them some poetical themes unknown to the Welsh. Two of the most celebrated heroes of the continental Breton romances, Lancelot and Tristan, do not figure in the *Mabinogion;* on the other hand, the characteristics of the Holy Grail are presented in a totally different way from that which we find in the French and German poets. A more attentive study shows that these elements, apparently added by the French poets, are in reality of Cymric origin. And first of all, M. de la Villemarqué has demonstrated to perfection that the name of Lancelot is only a translation of that of the Welsh hero Maël, who in point of fact exhibits the fullest analogy with the Lancelot of the French romances.[1] The context, the proper names, all the details of the romance of Lancelot also present the most pronounced Breton aspect. As much must be said of the romance of Tristan. It is even to be hoped that this curious legend will be discovered complete in some Welsh manuscript. Dr. Owen states that he has seen one of which he was unable to obtain a copy. As to the Holy Grail, it must be avowed that the mystic cup, the object after which the French *Parceval* and the German *Parsifal* go in search, has not nearly the same importance among the Welsh. In the romance of *Peredur* it only

[1] Ancelot is the diminutive of Ancel, and means servant, page, or esquire. To this day in the Cymric dialects Maël has the same signification. The surname of *Poursigant*, which we find borne by some Welshmen in the French service in the early part of the fourteenth century, is also no doubt a translation of Maël.

figures in an episodical fashion, and without a well-defined religious intention.

"Then Peredur and his uncle discoursed together, and he beheld two youths enter the hall, and proceed up to the chamber, bearing a spear of mighty size, with three streams of blood flowing from the point to the ground. And when all the company saw this, they began wailing and lamenting. But for all that, the man did not break off his discourse with Peredur. And as he did not tell Peredur the meaning of what he saw, he forbore to ask him concerning it. And when the clamour had a little subsided, behold two maidens entered, with a large salver between them, in which was a man's head, surrounded by a profusion of blood. And thereupon the company of the court made so great an outcry, that it was irksome to be in the same hall with them. But at length they were silent." This strange and wondrous circumstance remains an enigma to the end of the narrative. Then a mysterious young man appears to Peredur, apprises him that the lance from which the blood was dropping is that with which his uncle was wounded, that the vessel contains the blood and the head of one of his cousins, slain by the witches of Kerloiou, and that it is predestined that he, Peredur, should be their avenger. In point of fact, Peredur goes and convokes the Round Table; Arthur and his knights come and put the witches of Kerloiou to death.

If we now pass to the French romance of *Parceval*, we find that all this phantasmagoria clothes a very different significance. The lance is that with which Longus pierced Christ's side, the Grail or basin is that in which Joseph of Arimathea caught the divine blood. This miraculous vase procures all the good things of heaven and earth; it heals wounds, and is filled at the owner's pleasure with the most exquisite food. To approach it one must be in a state of grace; only a priest can tell of its marvels. To find these sacred relics after the passage of a thousand trials,—such is the object of Peredur's chivalry, at once worldly and mystical. In the end he becomes a priest; he takes the Grail and the lance into his hermitage; on the day of his death an angel bears them up to Heaven. Let us add that many traits prove that in the mind of the French *trouvère* the Grail is confounded with the eucharist. In the miniatures which occasionally accompany the romance of *Parceval*, the Grail is in the form of a pyx, appearing at all the solemn moments of the poem as a miraculous source of succour.

Is this strange myth, differing as it does from the simple narrative presented in the Welsh legend of *Peredur*, really Cymric, or ought we rather to see in it an original creation of the *trouvères*, based upon a Breton foundation? With M. de la Villemarqué[1] we believe that this curious fable is essentially Cymric. In the eighth century a Breton hermit had a vision of Joseph of Arimathea bearing the chalice of the Last Supper, and wrote the history called the *Gradal*. The whole Celtic mythology is full of the marvels of a magic caldron under which nine fairies blow silently, a mysterious vase which inspires poetic genius, gives wisdom, reveals the future, and unveils the secrets of the world. One day as Bran the Blessed was hunting in Ireland upon the shore of a lake, he saw come forth from it a black man bearing upon his back an enormous caldron, followed by a witch and a dwarf. This caldron was the instrument of the supernatural power of a family of giants. It cured all ills, and gave back life to the dead, but without restoring to them the use of speech—an allusion to the secret of the bardic initiation.

1 See the excellent discussion of this interesting problem in the introduction to *Contes populaires des anciens Bretons* (pp. 181 *et seq.*).

In the same way Perceval's wariness forms the whole plot of the quest of the Holy Grail. The Grail thus appears to us in its primitive meaning as the pass-word of a kind of freemasonry which survived in Wales long after the preaching of the Gospel, and of which we find deep traces in the legend of Taliessin. Christianity grafted its legend upon the mythological data, and a like transformation was doubtless made by the Cymric race itself. If the Welsh narrative of Peredur does not offer the same developments as the French romance of *Parceval*, it is because the Red Book of Hergest gives us an earlier version than that which served as a model for Chrétien de Troyes. It is also to be remarked that, even in *Parceval*, the mystical idea is not as yet completely developed, that the *trouvère* seems to treat this strange theme as a narrative which he has found already complete, and the meaning of which he can scarcely guess. The motive that sets Parceval a-field in the French romance, as well as in the Welsh version, is a family motive; he seeks the Holy Grail as a talisman to cure his uncle the Fisherman-King, in such a way that the religious idea is still subordinated to the profane intention. In the German version, on the other hand, full as it is of mysticism and theology, the Grail has a temple and priests. Parsifal, who has become a purely ecclesiastical hero, reaches the dignity of King of the Grail by his religious enthusiasm and his chastity.[1] Finally, the prose versions, more modern still, sharply distinguish the two chivalries, the one earthly, the other mystical. In them Parceval becomes the model of

[1] It is indeed remarkable that all the Breton heroes in their last transformation are at once gallant and devout. One of the most celebrated ladies of Arthur's court, Luned, becomes a saint and a martyr for her chastity, her festival being celebrated on August 1st. She it is who figures in the French romances under the name of Lunette. See Lady Guest, vol. i., pp. 113, 114.

the devout knight. This was the last of the metamorphoses which that all-powerful enchantress called the human imagination made him undergo; and it was only right that, after having gone through so many dangers, he should don a monkish frock, wherein to take his rest after his life of adventure.

V.

When we seek to determine the precise moment in the history of the Celtic races at which we ought to place ourselves in order to appreciate their genius in its entirety, we find ourselves led back to the sixth century of our era. Races have nearly always a predestined hour at which, passing from simplicity to reflection, they bring forth to the light of day, for the first time, all the treasures of their nature. For the Celtic races the poetic moment of awakening and primal activity was the sixth century. Christianity, still young amongst them, has not completely stifled the national cult; the religion of the Druids defends itself in its schools and holy places; warfare against the foreigner, without which a people never achieves a full consciousness of itself, attains its highest degree of spirit. It is the epoch of all the heroes of enduring fame, of all the characteristic saints of the Breton Church; finally, it is the great age of bardic literature, illustrious by the names of Taliessin, of Aneurin, of Liwarc'h Hên.

To such as would view critically the historical use of these half-fabulous names, and would hesitate to accept as authentic, poems that have come down to us through so long a series of ages, we reply that the objections raised to the antiquity of the bardic literature—objections of which W. Schlegel made himself the interpreter in opposition to M. Fauriel—have completely disappeared under the investigations of an enlightened and impartial criticism.[1] By a rare exception sceptical opinion has for once been found in the wrong. The sixth century is in fact for the Breton peoples a perfectly historical century. We touch this epoch of their history as closely and with as much certainty as Greek or Roman antiquity. It is indeed known that, up to a somewhat late period, the bards continued to compose pieces under the names—which had become popular—of Aneurin, Taliessin, and Liwarc'h Hên; but no confusion can be made between these insipid rhetorical exercises and the really ancient fragments which bear the names of the poets cited—fragments full of personal traits, local circumstances, and individual passions and feelings.

Such is the literature of which M. de la Villemarqué has attempted to unite the most ancient and authentic monuments in his *Breton Bards of the Sixth Century.* Wales has recognised the service that our learned compatriot has thus rendered to Celtic studies. We confess, however, to much preferring to the *Bards* the *Popular Songs of Brittany*. It is in the latter that M. de la Villemarqué has best served Celtic studies, by revealing to us a delightful literature, in which, more clearly than anywhere else, are apparent these features of gentleness, fidelity, resignation, and timid reserve which form the character of the Breton peoples.[2]

[1] This evidently does not apply to the language of the poems in question. It is well known that mediæval scribes, alien as they were to all ideas of archæology, modernised the texts, in measure as they copied them; and that a manuscript in the vulgar tongue, as a rule, only attests the language of him who transcribed it.

[2] This interesting collection ought not, however, to be accepted unreservedly; and the absolute confidence with which it has been quoted is not without its inconveniences. We believe that when M. de la Villemarqué comments on the fragments which, to his eternal honour, he has been the first to bring to light, his criticism is far from being proof against all reproach, and that several of the historical allusions

The theme of the poetry of the bards of the sixth century is simple and exclusively heroic; it ever deals with the great motives of patriotism and glory. There is a total absence of all tender feeling, no trace of love, no well-marked religious idea, but only a vague and naturalistic mysticism,—a survival of Druidic teaching,—and a moral philosophy wholly expressed in Triads, similar to that taught in the half-bardic, half-Christian schools of St. Cadoc and St. Iltud. The singularly artificial and highly wrought form of the style suggests the existence of a system of learned instruction possessing long traditions. A more pronounced shade, and there would be a danger of falling into a pedantic and mannered rhetoric. The bardic literature, by its lengthened existence through the whole of the Middle Ages, did not escape this danger. It ended by being no more than a somewhat insipid collection of unoriginalities in style, and conventional metaphors.[1]

The opposition between bardism and Christianity reveals itself in the pieces translated by M. de la Villemarqué by

which he considers that he finds in them are hypotheses more ingenious than solid. The past is too great, and has come down to us in too fragmentary a manner, for such coincidences to be probable. Popular celebrities are rarely those of history, and when the rumours of distant centuries come to us by two channels, one popular, the other historical, it is a rare thing for these two forms of tradition to be fully in accord with one another. M. de la Villemarqué is also too ready to suppose that the people repeats for centuries songs that it only half understands. When a song ceases to be intelligible, it is nearly always altered by the people, with the end of approximating it to the sounds familiar and significant to their ears. Is it not also to be feared that in this case the editor, in entire good faith, may lend some slight inflection to the text, so as to find in it the sense that he desires, or has in his mind?

[1] A Welsh scholar, Mr. Stephens, in his *History of Cymric Literature* (Llandovery, 1849), has demonstrated these successive transformations very well.

many features of original and pathetic interest. The strife which rent the soul of the old poets, their antipathy to the grey men of the monastery, their sad and painful conversion, are to be found in their songs. The sweetness and tenacity of the Breton character can alone explain how a heterodoxy so openly avowed as this maintained its position in face of the dominant Christianity, and how holy men, Kolumkill for example, took upon themselves the defence of the bards against the kings who desired to stamp them out. The strife was the longer in its duration, in that Christianity among the Celtic peoples never employed force against rival religions, and, at the worst, left to the vanquished the liberty of ill humour. Belief in prophets, indestructible among these peoples, created, in despite of faith, the Anti-Christian type of Merlin, and caused his acceptance by the whole of Europe. Gildas and the orthodox Bretons were ceaseless in their thunderings against the prophets, and opposed to them Elias and Samuel, two bards who only foretold good; even in the twelfth century Giraldus Cambrensis[1] saw a prophet in the town of Caerleon.

Thanks to this toleration bardism lasted into the heart of the Middle Ages, under the form of a secret doctrine, with a conventional language, and symbols almost wholly borrowed from the solar divinity of Arthur. This may be termed Neo-Druidism, a kind of Druidism subtilised and reformed on the model of Christianity, which may be seen growing more and more obscure and mysterious, until the moment of its total disappearance. A curious fragment belonging to this school, the dialogue between Arthur and Eliwlod, has transmitted to us the latest sighs of this latest protestation of expiring naturalism. Under the form of an

[1] See Note V.

eagle Eliwlod introduces the divinity to the sentiments of resignation, of subjection, and of humility, with which Christianity combated pagan pride. Hero-worship recoils step by step before the great formula, which Christianity ceases not to repeat to the Celtic races to sever them from their memories: There is none greater than God. Arthur allows himself to be persuaded to abdicate from his divinity, and ends by reciting the *Pater.*

I know of no more curious spectacle than this revolt of the manly sentiments of hero-worship against the feminine feeling which flowed so largely into the new faith. What, in fact, exasperates the old representatives of Celtic society are the exclusive triumph of the pacific spirit and the men, clad in linen and chanting psalms, whose voice is sad, who preach asceticism, and know the heroes no more.[1] We know the use that Ireland has made of this theme, in the dialogues which she loves to imagine between the representatives of her profane and religious life, Ossian and St. Patrick.[2] Ossian regrets the adventures, the chase, the blast of the horn, and the kings of old time. "If they were here," he says to St. Patrick, "thou should'st not thus be scouring the country with thy psalm-singing flock."

[1] The antipathy to Christianity attributed by the Armorican people to the dwarfs and *korigans* belongs in like measure to traditions of the opposition encountered by the Gospel in its beginnings. The *korigans* in fact are, for the Breton peasant, great princesses who would not accept Christianity when the apostles came to Brittany. They hate the clergy and the churches, the bells of which make them take to flight. The Virgin above all is their great enemy; she it is who has hounded them forth from their fountains, and on Saturday, the day consecrated to her, whosoever beholds them combing their hair or counting their treasures is sure to perish. (Villemarqué, *Chants populaires*, Introduction.)

[2] See Miss Brooke's *Reliques of Irish Poetry*, Dublin, 1789, pp. 37 *et seq.*, pp. 75 *et seq.*

Patrick seeks to calm him by soft words, and sometimes carries his condescension so far as to listen to his long histories, which appear to interest the saint but slightly. "Thou hast heard my story," says the old bard in conclusion; "albeit my memory groweth weak, and I am devoured with care, yet I desire to continue still to sing the deeds of yore, and to live upon ancient glories. Now am I stricken with years, my life is frozen within me, and all my joys are fleeting away. No more can my hand grasp the sword, nor mine arm hold the lance in rest. Among priests my last sad hour lengtheneth out, and psalms take now the place of songs of victory." "Let thy songs rest," says Patrick, "and dare not to compare thy Finn to the King of Kings, whose might knoweth no bounds: bend thy knees before Him, and know Him for thy Lord." It was indeed necessary to surrender, and the legend relates how the old bard ended his days in the cloister, among the priests whom he had so often used rudely, in the midst of these chants that he knew not. Ossian was too good an Irishman for any one to make up his mind to damn him utterly. Merlin himself had to cede to the new spell. He was, it is said, converted by St. Columba; and the popular voice in the ballads repeats to him unceasingly this sweet and touching appeal: "Merlin, Merlin, be converted; there is no divinity save that of God."

VI.

We should form an altogether inadequate idea of the physiognomy of the Celtic races, were we not to study them under what is perhaps the most singular aspect of their development—that is to say, their ecclesiastical antiquities and their saints. Leaving on one side the temporary repulsion which Christian mildness had to conquer in the classes of society which saw their influence diminished by the new order of things, it can be truly said, that the gentleness of manners and the exquisite sensibility of the Celtic races, in conjunction with the absence of a formerly existing religion of strong organisation, predestined them to Christianity. Christianity in fact, addressing itself by preference to the more humble feelings in human nature, met here with admirably prepared disciples; no race has so delicately understood the charm of littleness, none has placed the simple creature, the innocent, nearer God. The ease with which the new religion took possession of these peoples is also remarkable. Brittany and Ireland between them scarce count two or three martyrs; they are reduced to venerating as such those of their compatriots who were slain in the Anglo-Saxon and Danish invasions. Here comes to light the profound difference dividing the Celtic from the Teutonic race. The Teutons only received Christianity tardily and in spite of themselves, by scheming or by force, after a sanguinary resistance, and with terrible throes. Christianity was in fact on several sides repugnant to their nature; and one understands the regrets of pure Teutonists who, to this day, reproach the new faith with having corrupted their sturdy ancestors.

Such was not the case with the Celtic peoples; that gentle little race was naturally Christian. Far from changing them, and taking away some of their qualities, Christianity finished and perfected them. Compare the legends relating to the introduction of Christianity into the two countries, the *Kristni Saga* for instance, and the delightful legends of Lucius and St. Patrick. What a difference we find! In Iceland the first apostles are pirates, converted by some chance, now saying mass, now massacring their enemies, now resuming their former profession of sea-rovers; everything is done in accord with expediency, and without any serious faith. In Ireland and Brittany grace operates through women, by I know not what charm of purity and sweetness. The revolt of the Teutons was never effectually stifled; never did they forget the forced baptisms, and the sword-supported Carlovingian missionaries, until the day when Teutonism took its revenge, and Luther through seven centuries gave answer to Witikind. On the other hand, the Celts were, even in the third century, perfect Christians. To the Teutons Christianity was for long nothing but a Roman institution, imposed from without. They entered the Church only to trouble it; and it was not without very great difficulty that they succeeded in forming a national clergy. To the Celts, on the contrary, Christianity did not come from Rome; they had their native clergy, their own peculiar usages, their faith at first hand. It cannot, in fact, be doubted that in apostolic times Christianity was preached in Brittany; and several historians, not without justification, have considered that it was borne there by Judaistic Christians, or by disciples of the school of St. John. Everywhere else Christianity found, as a first substratum, Greek or Roman civilisation. Here it found a virgin soil of a nature analogous to its own, and naturally prepared to receive it.

Few forms of Christianity have offered an ideal of Christian perfection so pure as the Celtic Church of the sixth, seventh, and eighth centuries. Nowhere, perhaps, has God been better worshipped in spirit than in those great monastic communities of Hy, or of Iona, of Bangor, of Clonard, or of Lindisfarne. One of the most distinguished developments of Christianity—doubtless too distinguished for the popular and practical mission which the Church had to undertake—Pelagianism, arose from it. The true and refined morality, the simplicity, and the wealth of invention which give distinction to the legends of the Breton and Irish saints are indeed admirable. No race adopted Christianity with so much originality, or, while subjecting itself to the common faith, kept its national characteristics more persistently. In religion, as in all else, the Bretons sought isolation, and did not willingly fraternise with the rest of the world. Strong in their moral superiority, persuaded that they possessed the veritable canon of faith and religion, having received their Christianity from an apostolic and wholly primitive preaching, they experienced no need of feeling themselves in communion with Christian societies less noble than their own. Thence arose that long struggle of the Breton churches against Roman pretensions, which is so admirably narrated by M. Augustin Thierry,[1] thence those inflexible characters of Columba and the monks of Iona, defending their usages and institutions against the whole Church, thence finally the false position of the Celtic peoples in Catholicism, when that mighty force, grown more and more aggressive, had drawn them together from all quarters, and compelled their absorption in itself. Having no Catholic past, they found themselves unclassed on their entrance into the great family, and were never able to succeed in creating for themselves an Archbishopric. All their efforts and all their innocent deceits to attribute that title to the Churches of Dol and St. Davids were wrecked on the overwhelming divergence of their past; their bishops had to resign themselves to being obscure suffragans of Tours and Canterbury.

[1] In his History of the Conquest. The objections raised by M. Varin and some other scholars to M. Thierry's narrative only affect some secondary details, which were rectified in the edition published after the illustrious historian's death.

It remains to be said that, even in our own days, the powerful originality of Celtic Christianity is far from being effaced. The Bretons of France, although they have felt the consequences of the revolutions undergone by Catholicism on the Continent, are, at the present hour, one of the populations in which religious feeling has retained most independence. The new devotions find no favour with it; the people are faithful to the old beliefs and the old saints; the psalms of religion have for them an ineffable harmony. In the same way, Ireland keeps, in her more remote districts, quite unique forms of worship from those of the rest of the world, to which nothing in other parts of Christendom can be compared. The influence of modern Catholicism, elsewhere so destructive of national usages, has had here a wholly contrary effect, the clergy having found it incumbent on them to seek a vantage ground against Protestantism, in attachment to local practices and the customs of the past.

It is the picture of these Christian institutions, quite distinct from those of the remainder of the West, of this sometimes strange worship, of these legends of the saints marked with so distinct a seal of nationality, that lends an interest to the ecclesiastical antiquities of Ireland, of Wales, and of Armorican Brittany. No hagiology has remained more exclusively natural than that of the Celtic peoples; until the twelfth century those peoples admitted very few alien saints into their martyrology. None, too, includes so many naturalistic elements. Celtic Paganism offered so little resistance to the new religion, that the Church did not hold itself constrained to put in force against it the rigour with which elsewhere it pursued the slightest traces of mythology. The conscientious essay by W. Rees on the *Saints of Wales*, and that by the Rev.

John Williams, an extremely learned ecclesiastic of the diocese of St. Asaph, on the *Ecclesiastical Antiquities of the Cymry*, suffice to make one understand the immense value which a complete and intelligent history of the Celtic Churches, before their absorption in the Roman Church, would possess. To these might be added the learned work of Dom Lobineau on the *Saints of Brittany*, re-issued in our days by the Abbé Tresvaux, had not the half-criticism of the Benedictine, much worse than a total absence of criticism, altered those naïve legends and cut away from them, under the pretext of good sense and religious reverence, that which to us gives them interest and charm.

Ireland above all would offer a religious physiognomy quite peculiar to itself, which would appear singularly original, were history in a position to reveal it in its entirety. When we consider the legions of Irish saints who in the sixth, seventh, and eighth centuries inundated the Continent, and arrived from their isle bearing with them their stubborn spirit, their attachment to their own usages, their subtle and realistic turn of mind, and see the *Scots* (such was the name given to the Irish) doing duty, until the twelfth century, as instructors in grammar and literature to all the West, we cannot doubt that Ireland, in the first half of the Middle Ages, was the scene of a singular religious movement. Studious philologists and daring philosophers, the Hibernian monks were above all indefatigable copyists; and it was in part owing to them that the work of the pen became a holy task. Columba, secretly warned that his last hour is at hand, finishes the page of the psalter which he has commenced, writes at the foot that he bequeaths the continuation to his successor, and then goes into the church to die. Nowhere was monastic life to find such docile subjects. Credulous as a child, timid, indolent, inclined to submit and obey, the Irishman alone was capable of lending himself to that complete self-abdication in the hands of the abbot, which we find so deeply marked in the historical and legendary memorials of the Irish Church. One easily recognises the land where, in our own days, the priest, without provoking the slightest scandal, can, on a Sunday before quitting the altar, give the orders for his dinner in a very audible manner, and announce the farm where he intends to go and dine, and where he will hear his flock in confession. In the presence of a people which lived by imagination and the senses alone, the Church did not consider itself under the necessity of dealing severely with the caprices of religious fantasy. It permitted the free action of the popular instinct; and from this freedom emerged what is perhaps of all cults the most mythological and most analogous to the mysteries of antiquity, presented in Christian annals, a cult attached to certain places, and almost exclusively consisting in certain acts held to be sacramental.

Without contradiction the legend of St. Brandan is the most singular product of this combination of Celtic naturalism with Christian spiritualism. The taste of the Hibernian monks for making maritime pilgrimages through the archipelago of the Scottish and Irish seas, everywhere dotted with monasteries,[1] and the memory of yet more distant voyages in Polar seas, furnished the framework of this curious composition, so rich in local impressions. From Pliny (IV. xxx. 3) we learn that, even in his time, the

[1] The Irish saints literally covered the Western seas. A very considerable number of the saints of Brittany, St. Tenenan, St. Renan, etc., were emigrants from Ireland. The Breton legends of St. Malo, St. David, and of St. Pol of Léon are replete with similar stories of voyages to the distant isles of the West.

Bretons loved to venture their lives upon the high seas, in search of unknown isles. M. Letronne has proved that in 795, sixty-five years consequently before the Danes, Irish monks landed in Iceland and established themselves on the coast. In this island the Danes found Irish books and bells; and the names of certain localities still bear witness to the sojourn of those monks, who were known by the name of *Papæ* (fathers). In the Faröe Isles, in the Orkneys, and the Shetlands, indeed in all parts of the Northern seas, the Scandinavians found themselves preceded by those *Papæ*, whose habits contrasted so strangely with their own.[1] Did they not have a glimpse too of that great land, the vague memory of which seems to pursue them, and which Columbus was to discover, following the traces of their dreams? It is only known that the existence of an island, traversed by a great river and situated to the west of Ireland, was, on the faith of the Irish, a dogma for mediæval geographers.

The story went that, towards the middle of the sixth century, a monk called Barontus, on his return from voyaging upon the sea, came and craved hospitality at the monastery of Clonfert. Brandan the abbot besought him to give pleasure to the brothers by narrating *the marvels of God that he had seen on the high seas.* Barontus revealed to them the existence of an island surrounded by fogs, where he had left his disciple Mernoc; it is the *Land of Promise* that God keeps for his saints. Brandan with seventeen of his monks desired to go in quest of this mysterious land. They set forth in a leather boat, bearing with them as their sole provision a utensil of butter, wherewith to grease the hides of their craft. For seven years

[1] On this point see the careful researches of Humboldt in his *History of the Geography of the New Continent*, vol. ii.

they lived thus in their boat, abandoning to God sail and rudder, and only stopping on their course to celebrate the feasts of Christmas and Easter on the back of the king of fishes, Jasconius. Every step of this monastic Odyssey is a miracle, on every isle is a monastery, where the wonders of a fantastical universe respond to the extravagances of a wholly ideal life. Here is the *Isle of Sheep*, where these animals govern themselves according to their own laws; elsewhere the *Paradise of Birds*, where the winged race lives after the fashion of monks, singing matins and lauds at the canonical hours. Brandan and his companions celebrate mass here with the birds, and remain with them for fifty days, nourishing themselves with nothing but the singing of their hosts. Elsewhere there is the *Isle of Delight*, the ideal of monastic life in the midst of the seas. Here no material necessity makes itself felt; the lamps light of themselves for the offices of religion, and never burn out, for they shine with a spiritual light. An absolute stillness reigns in the island; every one knows precisely the hour of his death; one feels neither cold, nor heat, nor sadness, nor sickness of body or soul. All this has endured since the days of St. Patrick, who so ordained it. The *Land of Promise* is more marvellous still; there an eternal day reigns; all the plants have flowers, all the trees bear fruits. Some privileged men alone have visited it. On their return a perfume is perceived to come from them, which their garments keep for forty days.

In the midst of these dreams there appears with a surprising fidelity to truth the feeling for the picturesque in Polar voyages,—the transparency of the sea, the aspect of bergs and islands of ice melting in the sun, the volcanic phenomena of Iceland, the sporting of whales, the characteristic appearance of the Norwegian *fiords*, the sudden fogs, the sea calm as milk, the green isles crowned with grass which grows down to the very verge of the waves. This fantastical nature created expressly for another humanity, this strange topography at once glowing with fiction and speaking of truth, make the poem of St. Brandan one of the most extraordinary creations of the human mind, and perhaps the completest expression of the Celtic ideal. All is lovely, pure, and innocent; never has a gaze so benevolent and so gentle been cast upon the earth; there is not a single cruel idea, not a trace of frailty or repentance. It is the world seen through the crystal of a stainless conscience, one might almost say a human nature, as Pelagius wished it, that has never sinned. The very animals participate in this universal mildness. Evil appears under the form of monsters wandering on the deep, or of Cyclops confined in volcanic islands; but God causes them to destroy one another, and does not permit them to do hurt to the good.

We have just seen how, around the legend of a monk the Irish imagination grouped a whole cycle of physical and maritime myths. The *Purgatory of St. Patrick* became the framework of another series of fables, embodying the Celtic ideas concerning the other life and its different conditions.[1] Perhaps the profoundest instinct of the Celtic peoples is their desire to penetrate the unknown. With the sea before them, they wish to know what lies beyond; they dream of a Promised Land. In the face of the unknown that lies beyond the tomb, they dream of that great journey which the pen of Dante has celebrated. The legend tells how, while St. Patrick was preaching about Paradise and Hell to the Irish, they confessed that they would feel more assured of the reality of these places, if he would allow one

[1] See Thomas Wright's excellent dissertation, *Saint Patrick's Purgatory* (London, 1844), and Calderon's *The Well of Saint Patrick.*

of them to descend there, and then come back with information. St. Patrick consented. A pit was dug, by which an Irishman set out upon the subterranean journey. Others wished to attempt the journey after him. With the consent of the abbot of the neighbouring monastery, they descended into the shaft, they passed through the torments of Hell and Purgatory, and then each told of what he had seen. Some did not emerge again; those who did laughed no more, and were henceforth unable to join in any gaiety. Knight Owen made a descent in 1153, and gave a narrative of his travels which had a prodigious success.

Other legends related that when St. Patrick drove the goblins out of Ireland, he was greatly tormented in this place for forty days by legions of black birds. The Irish betook themselves to the spot, and experienced the same assaults which gave them an immunity from Purgatory. According to the narrative of Giraldus Cambrensis, the isle which served as the theatre of this strange superstition was divided into two parts. One belonged to the monks, the other was occupied by evil spirits, who celebrated religious rites in their own manner, with an infernal uproar. Some people, for the expiation of their sins, voluntarily exposed themselves to the fury of those demons. There were nine ditches in which they lay for a night, tormented in a thousand different ways. To make the descent it was necessary to obtain the permission of the bishop. His duty it was to dissuade the penitent from attempting the adventure, and to point out to him how many people had gone in who had never come out again. If the devotee persisted, he was ceremoniously conducted to the shaft. He was lowered down by means of a rope, with a loaf and a vessel of water to strengthen him in the combat against the fiend which he proposed to wage. On the following morning the sacristan offered the rope anew to the sufferer. If he mounted to the surface again, they brought him back to the church, bearing the cross and chanting psalms. If he were not to be found, the sacristan closed the door and departed. In more modern times pilgrims to the sacred isles spent nine days there. They passed over to them in a boat hollowed out of the trunk of a tree. Once a day they drank of the water of the lake; processions and stations were performed in the *beds* or *cells of the saints*. Upon the ninth day the penitents entered into the shaft. Sermons were preached to them warning them of the danger they were about to run, and they were told of terrible examples. They forgave their enemies and took farewell of one another, as though they were at their last agony. According to contemporary accounts, the shaft was a low and narrow kiln, into which nine entered at a time, and in which the penitents passed a day and a night, huddled and tightly pressed against one another. Popular belief imagined an abyss underneath, to swallow up the unworthy and the unbelieving. On emerging from the pit they went and bathed in the lake, and so their Purgatory was accomplished. It would appear from the accounts of eye-witnesses that, to this day, things happen very nearly after the same fashion.

The immense reputation of the Purgatory of St. Patrick filled the whole of the Middle Ages. Preachers made appeal to the public notoriety of this great fact, to controvert those who had their doubts regarding Purgatory. In the year 1358 Edward III. gave to a Hungarian of noble birth, who had come from Hungary expressly to visit the sacred well, letters patent attesting that he had undergone his Purgatory. Narratives of those travels beyond the tomb became a very fashionable form of literature; and it is important for us to remark the wholly mythological, and as wholly Celtic, characteristics dominant in them. It is in fact evident that we are dealing with a mystery or local cult, anterior to Christianity, and probably based upon the physical appearance of the country. The idea of Purgatory, in its final and concrete form, fared specially well amongst the Bretons and the Irish. Bede is one of the first to speak of it in a descriptive manner, and the learned Mr. Wright very justly observes that nearly all the descriptions of Purgatory come from Irishmen, or from Anglo-Saxons who have resided in Ireland, such as St. Fursey, Tundale, the Northumbrian Dryhthelm, and Knight Owen. It is likewise a remarkable thing that only the Irish were able to behold the marvels of their Purgatory. A canon from Hemstede in Holland, who descended in 1494, saw nothing at all. Evidently this idea of travels in the other world and its infernal categories, as the Middle Ages accepted it, is Celtic. The belief in the three circles of existence is again to be found in the *Triads*,[1] under an aspect which does not permit one to see any Christian interpolation.

The soul's peregrinations after death are also the favourite theme of the most ancient Armorican poetry. Among the features by which the Celtic races most impressed the Romans were the precision of their ideas upon the future life, their inclination to suicide, and the loans and contracts which they signed with the other world in view. The more frivolous peoples of the South saw with awe in this assurance the fact of a mysterious race, having an under-

[1] A series of aphorisms under the form of triplets, which give us, with numerous interpolations, the ancient teaching of the bards, and that traditional wisdom which, according to the testimony of the ancients, was transmitted by means of mnemonic verses in the schools of the Druids.

standing of the future and the secret of death. Through the whole of classical antiquity runs the tradition of an Isle of Shadows, situated on the confines of Brittany, and of a folk devoted to the passage of souls, which lives upon the neighbouring coast. In the night they hear dead men prowling about their cabin, and knocking at the door. Then they rise up; their craft is laden with invisible beings; on their return it is lighter. Several of these features reproduced by Plutarch, Claudian, Procopius, and Tzetzes [1] would incline one to believe that the renown of the Irish myths made its way into classical antiquity about the first or second century. Plutarch, for example, relates, concerning the Cronian Sea, fables identical with those which fill the legend of St. Malo. Procopius, describing the sacred Island of Brittia, which consists of two parts separated by the sea, one delightful, the other given over to evil spirits, seems to have read in advance the description of the *Purgatory of St. Patrick*, which Giraldus Cambrensis was to give seven centuries later. It cannot be doubted for a moment, after the able researches of Messrs. Ozanam, Labitte, and Wright, that to the number of poetical themes which Europe owes to the genius of the Celts, is to be added the framework of the Divine Comedy.

One can understand how greatly this invincible attraction to fables must have discredited the Celtic race in the eyes of nationalities that believed themselves to be more serious. It is in truth a strange thing, that the whole of the mediæval epoch, whilst submitting to the influence of the Celtic imagination, and borrowing from Brittany and Ireland at least half of its poetical subjects, believed itself obliged, for the saving of its own honour, to slight and satirise the people to which it owed them. Even Chrétien de Troyes,

[1] See Note VI.

for example, who passed his life in exploiting the Breton romances for his own purposes, originated the saying—

> "Les Gallois sont tous par nature
> Plus sots que bêtes de pâture."

Some English chronicler, I know not who, imagined he was making a charming play upon words when he described those beautiful creations, the whole world of which deserved to live, as "the childish nonsense with which those *brutes* of *Bretons* amuse themselves." The Bollandists[1] found it incumbent to exclude from their collection, as apocryphal extravagances, those admirable religious legends, with which no Church has anything to compare. The decided leaning of the Celtic race towards the ideal, its sadness, its fidelity, its good faith, caused it to be regarded by its neighbours as dull, foolish, and superstitious. They could not understand its delicacy and refined manner of feeling. They mistook for awkwardness the embarrassment experienced by sincere and open natures in the presence of more artificial natures. The contrast between French frivolity and Breton stubbornness above all led, after the fourteenth century, to most deplorable conflicts, whence the Bretons ever emerged with a reputation for wrong-headedness.

It was still worse, when the nation that most prides itself on its practical good sense found confronting it the people that, to its own misfortune, is least provided with that gift. Poor Ireland, with her ancient mythology, with her Purgatory of St. Patrick, and her fantastic travels of St. Brandan, was not destined to find grace in the eyes of English puritanism. One ought to observe the disdain of English critics for these fables, and their superb pity for the Church

[1] See Note VII.

which dallies with Paganism, so far as to keep up usages which are notoriously derived from it. Assuredly we have here a praiseworthy zeal, arising from natural goodness; and yet, even if these flights of imagination did no more than render a little more supportable many sufferings which are said to have no remedy, that after all would be something. Who shall dare to say where, here on earth, is the boundary between reason and dreaming? Which is worth more, the imaginative instinct of man, or the narrow orthodoxy that pretends to remain rational, when speaking of things divine? For my own part, I prefer the frank mythology, with all its vagaries, to a theology so paltry, so vulgar, and so colourless, that it would be wronging God to believe that, after having made the visible world so beautiful he should have made the invisible world so prosaically reasonable.

In presence of the ever-encroaching progress of a civilisation which is of no country, and can receive no name, other than that of modern or European, it would be puerile to hope that the Celtic race is in the future to succeed in obtaining isolated expression of its originality. And yet we are far from believing that this race has said its last word. After having put in practice all chivalries, devout and worldly, gone with Peredur in quest of the Holy Grail and fair ladies, and dreamed with St. Brandan of mystical Atlantides, who knows what it would produce in the domain of intellect, if it hardened itself to an entrance into the world, and subjected its rich and profound nature to the conditions of modern thought? It appears to me that there would result from this combination, productions of high originality, a subtle and discreet manner of taking life, a singular union of strength and weakness, of rude simplicity and mildness. Few races have had so complete a poetic childhood as the Celtic; mythology, lyric poetry, epic, romantic imagination, religious enthusiasm—none of these failed them; why should reflection fail them? Germany, which commenced with science and criticism, has come to poetry; why should not the Celtic races, which began with poetry, finish with criticism? There is not so great a distance from one to the other as is supposed; the poetical races are the philosophic races, and at bottom philosophy is only a manner of poetry When one considers how Germany, less than a century ago, had her genius revealed to her, how a multitude of national individualities, to all appearance effaced, have suddenly risen again in our own days, more instinct with life than ever, one feels persuaded that it is a rash thing to lay down any law on the intermittence and awakening of nations; and that modern civilisation, which appeared to be made to absorb them, may perhaps be nothing more than their united fruition.

WHAT IS A NATION?[1]

I PROPOSE to analyse with you an idea, simple in appearance, but capable of the most dangerous misunderstanding. The forms of human society are of the most varied types. Great conglomerations of people, as in the case of China, of Egypt, of ancient Babylon; the tribe, as in the case of the Hebrews and the Arabs; the city, as in the case of Athens and Sparta; unions of different countries, in the fashion of the Empire of Achæmenes, the Roman Empire, or the Carlovingian Empire; communities of no country, held together by the bond of religion, like the Israelites or the Parsees; nations like France, England, and the majority of modern European autonomies; confederations, as in the case of Switzerland and America; relationships similar to those which race and, in a greater degree, language establish between the different branches of the Teutonic family, the different branches of the Slavs;—these are modes of grouping which all exist, or at least have existed, and which cannot be confounded, the one with the other, without the most serious inconvenience. At the time of the French Revolution there was a belief that the institutions of small independent towns, such as Sparta and Rome, could be applied to our great nations of thirty or forty millions of souls. In our own day a still graver error is committed: the race is confounded with the nation, and

[1] A lecture delivered at the Sorbonne, March 11th, 1882.

to racial, or rather to linguistic groups, is attributed a sovereignty analogous to that of really existent peoples. Let us attempt to arrive at some precision in these difficult questions, where the least confusion in the sense of words, at the beginning of the discussion, may produce in the end the most fatal errors. What we are about to undertake is a delicate task; it is almost vivisection. We are to deal with living men, as, under ordinary circumstances, the dead alone are treated. In doing so we shall use coolness, and the most absolute impartiality.

I.

Since the end of the Roman Empire, or rather since the disruption of the Empire of Charlemagne, Western Europe appears to us divided into nations, of which some, at certain epochs, have sought to exercise a supremacy over others, without any lasting success. What Charles V., Louis XIV, and Napoleon I. were unable to do in the past, is hardly likely to be achieved by any one in the future. The establishment of a new Roman Empire, or a new Carlovingian Empire, has become an impossibility. Europe is too deeply divided for an attempt at universal dominion not to provoke, and that quickly, a coalition which would force the ambitious nation to retire within its natural bounds. A species of equilibrium has long been in existence. France, England, Germany, and Russia will still be, in centuries to come, and in spite of the vicissitudes they will have gone through, historic individualities, essential pieces of a chess-board, the squares of which vary unceasingly in importance and greatness, but are never altogether confused.

Nations, understood in this way, are a new feature in

history. Antiquity knew them not; Egypt, China, ancient Chaldea, were to no extent nations. There were flocks led by a son of the Sun, or a son of Heaven. There were no Egyptian citizens, as there are no Chinese citizens. Classical antiquity had republics, and municipal kingdoms, confederations of neighbouring republics, and empires; it scarcely had the nation, in the sense in which we understand it. Athens, Sparta, Sidon, and Tyre were little centres of admirable patriotism; but they were cities with a comparatively restricted territory. Gaul, Spain, and Italy, before their absorption in the Roman Empire, were clusters of peoples, often in league with one another, but unpossessed of central institutions or dynasties. Nor were even the Assyrian Empire, the Persian Empire, or that of Alexander, nations. There were never Assyrian patriots; the Persian Empire was one vast feudality. Not a single nation traces its origin to the colossal enterprise of Alexander, which was nevertheless so pregnant with consequences for the general history of civilisation.

The Roman Empire was much nearer to being a nation. In return for the immense boon of the cessation of wars, the Roman dominion, at first so painful, was very quickly loved. It was a great association, synonymous with order, peace, and civilisation. In the later days of the Empire there was among the greater minds, among enlightened bishops, and among the lettered, a genuine feeling for "the Roman Peace," as opposed to the menacing chaos of barbarism. But an Empire twelve times greater in extent than the France of the present day could not form a state in the modern acceptance of the term. The severance of East and West was inevitable. The attempts at a Gaulish Empire in the third century were unsuccessful. It was the Teutonic invasion that introduced into the world the principle which, later, served as a basis to the existence of nationalities.

What, in fact, were those Teutonic peoples doing, from their great invasions of the fifth century to the last Norman conquests in the tenth? They changed the essential character of races only slightly; but they imposed dynasties and a military aristocracy upon more or less considerable portions of the former Empire of the West, which took the name of their invaders. Thence arose a France, a Burgundy, a Lombardy—later still, a Normandy. The rapid preponderance assumed by the Frankish Empire revived for a moment the unity of the West; but that Empire was shattered irremediably towards the middle of the ninth century, the treaty of Verdun traced divisions immutable in principle; and thenceforward France, Germany, England, Italy, and Spain journeyed by ways, often circuitous, and through a thousand vicissitudes, to their full national existence, such as we see flourishing to-day.

What, then, is the characteristic feature of these different states? It consists in the fusion of the populations which compose them. In the countries that we have just enumerated, there is nothing analogous to what you will find in Turkey, where the Turk, the Slav, the Greek, the Armenian, the Arab, the Syrian, and the Kurd are as distinct now as on the day of their conquest. Two essential circumstances contributed to bring this result to pass. First of all is the fact, that the Teutonic tribes adopted Christianity as soon as they had had relations of some little duration with the Greek and Latin peoples. When conqueror and conquered are of the same religion, or rather when the conqueror adopts the religion of the conquered, the Turkish system, the absolute distinction of men according to their respective faiths, can no longer be possible.

The second circumstance was the conquerors' forgetfulness of their own language. The grandsons of Clovis, of Alaric, of Gondebaud, of Alboin, and of Rollo were already speaking Romance. This fact was itself the consequence of another important peculiarity, namely, that the Franks, the Burgundians, the Goths, the Lombards, and the Normans had very few women of their own race with them. For several generations the chiefs espoused only Teutonic women; but their concubines were Latin, the nurses of their children were Latin; the whole tribe married Latin women. And so it was that the *Lingua Francica* and the *Lingua Gothica* had a very short existence, after the settlement of the Franks and Goths in Roman territories. The same was not the case in England, for there can be no doubt that the Anglo-Saxon invaders had women with them; the ancient British population took to flight; and, moreover, Latin was no longer dominant in Britain, indeed it had never been so. Even if Gaulish had been generally spoken in Gaul in the fifth century, Clovis and his followers would not have abandoned Teutonic for it.

From this ensues the important fact, that in spite of the extreme violence of the manners of the Teutonic invaders, the mould that they imposed became, in the course of centuries, the very mould of the nation. France, very legitimately, came to be the name of a country into which only an imperceptible minority of Franks had entered. In the tenth century, in the earliest *Chansons de Geste*, which are such a perfect mirror of the spirit of the age, all the inhabitants of France are Frenchmen. The idea of a difference of races in the population of France, that is so apparent in Gregory of Tours,[1] is not present to any extent in the French writers and poets, posterior to Hugh Capet.

[1] See Note VIII.

5

The difference between noble and serf is as accentuated as it well can be; but in no respect is the difference an ethnical one; it is a difference in courage, in habits, and in hereditarily transmitted education. The idea, that the beginning of it all may be a conquest, does not occur to anybody. The fictitious theories, according to which nobility owed its origin to a privilege, conferred by the king for great services rendered to the state, to such an extent that all nobility is an acquisition, were established as a dogma in the thirteenth century. The same thing was the sequel of nearly all the Norman conquests. At the end of one or two generations, the Norman invaders were no longer to be distinguished from the rest of the population. Their influence had not been the less profound; to the conquered land they had given a nobility, warlike habits, and a patriotism hitherto unexistent.

Forgetfulness, and I shall even say historical error, form an essential factor in the creation of a nation; and thus it is that the progress of historical studies may often be dangerous to the nationality. Historical research, in fact, brings back to light the deeds of violence that have taken place at the commencement of all political formations, even of those the consequences of which have been most beneficial. Unity is ever achieved by brutality. The union of Northern and Southern France was the result of an extermination, and of a reign of terror that lasted for nearly a hundred years. The king of France who was, if I may say so, the ideal type of a secular crystalliser, the king of France who made the most perfect national unity in existence, lost his prestige when seen at too close a distance. The nation that he had formed cursed him; and to-day the knowledge of what he was worth, and what he did, belongs only to the cultured.

It is by contrast that these great laws of the history of Western Europe become apparent. In the undertaking which the King of France, in part by his tyranny, in part by his justice, achieved so admirably, many countries came to disaster. Under the crown of St. Stephen, Magyars and Slavs have remained as distinct as they were eight hundred years ago. Far from combining the different elements in its dominions, the house of Hapsburg has held them apart, and often opposed to one another. In Bohemia the Czech element and the German element are superimposed like oil and water in a glass. The Turkish policy of separation of nationalities according to religion has had much graver results. It has brought about the ruin of the East. Take a town like Smyrna or Salonica; you will find there five or six communities, each with its own memories, and possessing among them scarcely anything in common. But the essence of a nation is, that all its individual members should have many things in common; and also, that all of them should hold many things in oblivion. No French citizen knows whether he is a Burgundian, an Alan, or a Visgoth; every French citizen ought to have forgotten St. Bartholomew, and the massacres of the South in the thirteenth century. There are not ten families in France able to furnish proof of a French origin; and yet, even if such a proof were given, it would be essentially defective, in consequence of a thousand unknown crosses, capable of deranging all genealogical systems.

The modern nation is then the historical result of a series of events, converging in the same direction. Sometimes unity has been achieved by a dynasty, as in the case of France; sometimes by the direct will of the provinces, as in the case of Holland, Switzerland, and Belgium; sometimes by a general feeling slowly vanquishing the caprices of feudality, as in the case of Italy and Germany. But a profound *raison d'être* has always governed these formations. The principles in such cases come to light in the most unexpected ways. In our own times we have seen Italy united by her defeats, and Turkey destroyed by her victories. Every defeat advanced the cause of Italy, every victory was a loss to Turkey; for Italy is a nation, Turkey, outside Asia Minor, is not. It is the glory of France to have proclaimed by the French Revolution that a nation exists by itself. We ought not to complain because we find ourselves imitated. Ours is the principle of nations. But what then is a nation? Why is Holland a nation, while Hanover or the Grand Duchy of Parma is not? How does France persist in being a nation, when the principle which created her has disappeared? How is Switzerland, with three languages, two religions, and three or four races, a nation, while Tuscany, for example, which is homogeneous, is not? Why is Austria a state and not a nation? In what respect does the principle of nationality differ from the principle of races? These are the points upon which a reflective mind must be fixed, if it is to find a satisfactory solution. The affairs of the world are scarcely regulated by such reasoning; but serious students wish to carry into such matters a certain amount of reason, and to unravel the confusions in which superficial minds entangle themselves.

II.

In the opinion of certain political theorists a nation is, before all else, a dynasty representing an ancient conquest, a conquest first accepted and then forgotten by the mass of the people. According to the politicians of whom I speak, the grouping of provinces effected by a dynasty, by its wars, by its marriages, or by its treaties, comes to an end with the dynasty which has formed it. It is very true that the majority of modern nations owe their existence to a family of feudal origin, which contracted a marriage with the soil, and was in some measure a nucleus of centralisation. There was nothing natural or necessary about the boundaries of France in 1789. The large zone that the house of Capet added to the narrow limits of the Treaty of Verdun, was in every sense the personal acquisition of that house. At the time when the annexations were made, there was no idea of natural frontiers, or of the rights of nations, or of the will of the provinces. The union of England, Ireland, and Scotland was in like manner a dynastic act. The reason for Italy delaying so long in becoming a nation was that no one of her numerous reigning houses, before the present century, made itself the centre of unity. And it is a strange thing that it is from the obscure island of Sardinia, from territory scarcely Italian, that she has taken a royal title.[1] Holland, which created herself by an act of heroic resolution, has nevertheless contracted a marriage with the house of Orange, and would run real dangers on the day of that union's being compromised.

But is such a law as this absolute? Certainly not. Switzerland and the United States, conglomerations formed by successive additions, have no dynastic base. I shall not discuss the question with regard to France. It would be necessary to have the secret of the future. Let us only say that the great royal house of France had been so highly national, that, on the morrow of its fall, the nation was able to stand without its support. And then the

[1] The House of Savoy only owes its royal title to the possession of Sardinia (1720).

eighteenth century had changed everything. Man had returned, after centuries of abasement, to the old spirit, to self-respect, to the idea of his rights. The words "country" and "citizen" had resumed their significance. Thus it was that the boldest operation ever attempted in history was accomplished—an operation which might be compared to what in physiology would be the gift of life and its first identity, to a body from which head and heart had been removed.

It must then be admitted that a nation can exist without a dynastic principle; and even that nations formed by dynasties can separate themselves from them without, for that reason, ceasing to exist. The old principle, which held account of no right but that of princes, can no longer be maintained; above the dynastic right there is the national right. On what foundation shall we build up this national right, by what sign shall we know it, from what tangible fact shall we derive it?

(I.) From race, say several with assurance. Artificial divisions resulting from feudality, royal marriages, or diplomatic congresses, are unstable. What does remain firm and fixed is the race of populations. That it is which constitutes right and legitimacy. The Teutonic family, for example, according to this theory, has the right of reclaiming such of its members as are beyond the pale of Teutonism—even when these members do not seek reunion. The right of Teutonism over such a province is greater than the right of the inhabitants of the province over themselves. Thus is created a kind of primordial right, analogous to that of the divine right of kings; for the principle of nations is substituted that of ethnography. This is a very grave error, which, if it became dominant, would cause the ruin of European civilisation. So far as the national principle is just and legitimate, so far is the primordial right of races narrow, and full of danger for true progress.

It may be admitted that, in the tribe and the city of antiquity, the fact of race had an importance of the highest order. But the ancient tribe and city were only extensions of the family. In Sparta and in Athens all the citizens were more or less closely related. It was the same in the Beni-Israel,[1] it is so to this day among the Arab tribes. From Athens, from Sparta, from the Israelite tribe, let us now turn to the Roman Empire. The situation is altogether different. Founded by violence, then maintained by self-interest, this great agglomeration of towns, and altogether diverse provinces, dealt a blow of the gravest kind to the idea of race. Christianity, with its universal and absolute character, tended still more efficiently in the same direction. It entered into a close alliance with the Roman Empire, and the effect of those two incomparable agents of unity was to banish ethnographical reason for centuries from the government of human affairs.

The barbarian invasion was, despite appearances, a step further in the same direction. There was nothing racial in the division of barbaric kingdoms; they were governed by the force or the caprice of the invaders. The race of the populations that they subjugated was, for them, a matter of the greatest indifference. Charlemagne achieved again, in his own way, what Rome had achieved already: a single empire composed of the most diverse races. The authors of the Treaty of Verdun, when they traced imperturbably their two great lines from North to South, had not the slightest care for the race of the peoples on either side. The changes of frontier, which took place later than the Middle Ages, were also free from all racial considerations.

[1] See Note IX.

If the continuous policy of the house of Capet succeeded in grouping together, under the name of France, almost all the territories of ancient Gaul, we do not have there an effect of the tendencies that those countries should have had, to rejoin their own congeners. The Dauphiny, Bresse, Provence, the Franche-Comté, no longer had memories of a common origin. All Gaulish feeling had perished in the second century of our era; and it is only by the eyes of erudition that, in our own days, the individuality of the Gaulish character has been retrospectively found once more.

Racial considerations have then been for nothing in the constitution of modern nations. France is Celtic, Iberian, Teutonic. Germany is Teutonic, Celtic, and Slavonic. Italy is the country where ethnography is most confused. Gauls, Etruscans, Pelasgians, and Greeks, to say nothing of many other elements, are crossed in an undecipherable medley. The British Isles, as a whole, exhibit a mixture of Celtic and Teutonic blood, the relative proportions of which it is singularly difficult to define.

The truth is that there is no pure race; and that making politics depend upon ethnographical analysis, is allowing it to be borne upon a chimæra. The most noble countries, England, France, Italy, are those where blood is most mingled. Is Germany an exception to this rule? Is she purely Teutonic? What an illusion is this! The whole of the South was once Gaulish. The whole of the East beyond the Elbe is Slavonic. And what, in point of fact, are the parts alleged to be really pure? Here we touch on one of the problems concerning which it is most important to have our ideas clear, and to avoid misunderstandings.

Discussions upon race are interminable, because the word "race" is taken by the philological historians and by physiological anthropologists in two totally different senses. For the anthropologists race has the same meaning as it has in zoology; it indicates a real descent, a relationship by blood. But the study of languages and history does not lead to the same classifications as physiology. The words *Brachycephalus* and *Dolichocephalus* have no place in history or philology. In the human group, that created the Aryan languages and customs, there were already *Brachycephali* and *Dolichocephali.* The same must be said of the primitive group, that created the languages and institutions known as Semitic. In other words, the zoological origins of humanity are enormously anterior to the origins of culture, civilisation, and language. The primitive Aryan, primitive Semitic, and primitive Tauranian groups, had no physiological unity. These groupings are historical facts which took place at a certain epoch—let us say fifteen or twenty thousand years ago—while the zoological origin of man is lost in incalculable mystery. What is philologically and historically called the Teutonic race, is assuredly a very distinct family of the human species. But is it a family in the anthropological sense? Certainly not; the appearance of the Teutonic individuality in history only took place a very few centuries before the Christian era. Apparently the Teutons had not emerged from the earth up to that time. Before it, mingled as they were with the Slavs in the great indistinct mass of the Scythians, they had no individuality of their own. An Englishman is a distinct type in the aggregate of humanity. But the type of what is very improperly called the Anglo-Saxon race[1] is neither

[1] The Teutonic element is not much more considerable in the United Kingdom than it was in France, at the time when she possessed Alsace and Metz. The Teutonic tongue dominated in the British Isles, simply because Latin had not entirely supplanted the Celtic idioms, as it had done among the Gauls.

the Briton of the time of Cæsar, nor the Anglo-Saxon of Hengist, nor the Dane of Knut, nor the Norman of William the Conqueror; it is the product of them all. The Frenchman is neither a Gaul, nor a Frank, nor a Burgundian. He is that which has come out of the great caldron, where, under the governance of the King of France, the most various elements have fermented together. An inhabitant of Jersey or Guernsey differs in nothing, as regards origin, from the Norman population of the neighbouring coast. In the eleventh century, the most penetrative vision could not have detected the slightest difference between the two sides of the channel. From insignificant circumstances, it happened that Philip Augustus did not take these islands with the rest of Normandy. Separated for nearly seven hundred years, the two populations have become, not only foreign to one another, but unlike in every respect. Race, as we historians understand it, is then something that makes and unmakes itself. The study of race is of capital importance to the student who occupies himself with the history of mankind. It has no application in politics. The instinctive consciousness which presided over the construction of the map of Europe took no account of race; and the greatest European nations are nations of essentially mixed blood.

Racial facts then, important as they are in the beginning, have a constant tendency to lose their importance. Human history is essentially different from zoology. Race is not everything, as it is in the case of the rodents and felines; and we have no right to go about the world feeling the heads of people, then taking them by the throat, and saying, "You are of our blood; you belong to us!" Beyond anthropological characteristics there are reason, justice, truth, and beauty; and these are the same in all.

Nay, this ethnographical politics is not even safe. You exploit it to-day on other people; some day you may see it turned against yourselves. Is it certain that the Germans, who have raised the flag of ethnography so high, will not see the Slavs coming to analyse in their turn the names of villages in Saxony and Lusatia, to seek for traces of the Wilzen or the Obotrites, and to ask account of the massacres and slavery which their ancestors suffered at the hands of the Othos? It is good for all to know how to forget. I have a great liking for ethnography; it is a science of rare interest; but because I wish to see it free, I wish it to be without political application. In ethnography, as in all studies, systems change; it is the condition of progress. Should then nations change with the systems also? If so, the frontiers of states would follow the fluctuations of science. Patriotism would depend on a more or less paradoxical dissertation. They would come to the patriot and say, "You are deceived; you have been shedding your blood for such and such a cause; you believed yourself to be a Celt, while, as a matter of fact, you are a Teuton." And then, ten years afterwards, they would come and tell him that he was a Slav. To avoid falsifying science, let us abstain from giving advice upon these problems, in which so many interests are involved. You may be sure that if science is charged with the duty of furnishing the elements of diplomacy, it will be, in many cases, found to be in the gravest error. It has better work to do; let us simply demand of it the truth.

(II.) What we have been saying about race must also be said of language. Language invites re-union; it does not force it. The United States and England, Spanish America and Spain, speak the same languages, and do not form single nations. On the contrary, Switzerland, which owes her stability to the fact that she was founded by the assent of her several parts, counts three or four languages. In man there is something superior to language,—will. The will of Switzerland to be united, in spite of the variety of her languages, is a much more important fact than a similarity of language, often obtained by persecution.

It is an honourable fact for France, that she has never sought to procure unity of speech by measures of coercion. Can we not have the same feelings and thoughts, and love the same things in different languages? We were speaking just now of the inconvenience of making international politics depend on ethnography. There would not be less in making politics depend on comparative philology. Let us allow the fullest liberty of discussion to these interesting studies; do not let us mingle them with that which would affect their serenity. The political importance attached to languages results from the way in which they are regarded as signs of race. Nothing can be more incorrect. Prussia, where nothing but German is now spoken, spoke Slavonic a few centuries ago; Wales speaks English; Gaul and Spain speak the primitive idiom of Alba Longa; Egypt speaks Arabic; indeed, examples are innumerable. Even at the beginning similarity of speech did not imply similarity of race. Let us take the proto-Aryan or proto-Semitic tribe; there were to be found slaves accustomed to speak the same language as their masters; but nevertheless the slave was then very often of a different race from that of his master. Let us repeat it; these classifications of the Indo-European, Semitic, and other tongues, created with such admirable sagacity by comparative philology, do not coincide with the classifications of anthropology. Languages are historical formations, which give but little indication of the blood of those who speak them; and, in any case, cannot enchain human liberty, when there is a question of determining the family with which we unite ourselves for life and death.

The exclusive consideration of language has, like the unduly great attention given to race, its dangers and its drawbacks. When we thus exaggerate it, we imprison ourselves in a limited culture, held as being national; we are hemmed in, cooped up. We quit the great atmosphere that we breathe in the vast field of humanity, to shut ourselves up in conventicles of compatriots. Nothing can be worse for the mind, nothing more hurtful to civilisation. Do not let us abandon this fundamental principle, that man is a reasonable and moral being before being allotted to such and such a language, before being a member of such and such a race, an adherent of such and such a culture. Before French culture, German culture, Italian culture, there is human culture. Consider the great men of the Renaissance; they were neither French, nor Italian, nor German. They had found anew, by their intercourse with antiquity, the secret of the true education of the human mind; to it they devoted themselves body and soul; and they did well!

(III.) Nor can religion offer a sufficient basis for the establishment of a modern nationality. In the beginning religion was essential to the very existence of the social group. The social group was an extension of the family. Religious rites were family rites. The Athenian religion was the cult of Athens itself, of its mythical founders, of its laws and customs. It implied no dogmatic theology. This religion was in every sense of the term a State religion. If any one refused to practise it, he was no longer an Athenian. In reality it was the worship of the personified Acropolis. To swear on the altar of Agraulos was to take an oath to die for one's country. This religion was the equivalent of what drawing lots for military service, or the cult of the flag, is among us. To refuse to participate in such a worship was like a refusal of military service in our modern societies. It was a declaration that one was not an Athenian. From another point of view, it is clear that such a religion had no force for any one who was not an Athenian; and thus no proselytism was exercised to compel aliens to accept it. The slaves in Athens did not practise it. The same thing held good in some small mediæval republics. A man was not a good Venetian if he did not swear by St. Mark; he was not a good citizen of Amalfi if he did not place St. Andrew above all the other saints of Paradise. In those small communities tyranny, which in later days meant persecution, was legitimate, and of as little consequence as our own fashion of keeping the birthday of the father of the family, and addressing our good wishes to him on New Year's day.

What was right at Sparta and Athens was already no longer so in the kingdoms that originated in Alexander's conquest; above all, was no longer right in the Roman Empire. The persecutions of Antiochus Epiphanes,[1] for the purpose of forcing the worship of the Olympian Jupiter on the East, those of the Roman Empire for the purpose of keeping up a pseudo-State religion, were a mistake, a crime, a veritable absurdity. In our own days the position is perfectly clear. No longer are there masses of people professing a uniform belief. Every one believes and practises after his own fashion, what he can, as he pleases. The state-religion is a thing of the past. One can be a Frenchman, an Englishman, or a German; and at the same time be a Catholic, a Protestant, or a Jew, or else be of no

[1] See Note X.

creed at all. Religion has become a matter for the individual; it affects the individual's conscience alone. The division of nations into Catholic and Protestant no longer exists. Religion, which fifty-two years ago was so considerable an element in the formation of Belgium, retains all its importance in the spiritual jurisdiction of each man; but it has almost completely disappeared from the considerations that trace the limits of peoples.

(IV.) Community of interests is assuredly a powerful bond between men. But nevertheless can interests suffice to make a nation? I do not believe it. Community of interests makes commercial treaties. There is a sentimental side to nationality; it is at once body and soul; a *Zollverein* is not a fatherland.

(V.) Geography, or what we may call natural frontiers, certainly plays a considerable part in the division of nations. Geography is one of the essential factors of history. Rivers have carried races forward; mountains have checked them. The former have favoured, the latter limited, historic movements. Can it be said, however, that, as certain persons believe, the boundaries of a nation are inscribed upon the map; and that this nation has a right to judge what is necessary, to round off certain contours, to reach some mountain or river, to which a species of *a priori* faculty of limitation is ascribed? I know of no doctrine more arbitrary, or more disastrous. By it all violence is justified. First, let us ask, do mountains or rivers constitute these so-called natural frontiers? It is incontestable that mountains separate; but, on the other hand, rivers unite. And then all mountains cannot cut off states. Which are those that separate, and those that do not separate? From Biarritz to the Tornea there is not a single river-estuary which, more than another, has the character of a boundary.

Had history required it, the Loire, the Seine, the Meuse, the Elbe, and the Oder would have, to the same extent as the Rhine, that character of a natural frontier which has caused so many infractions of the fundamental right,—the will of men. Strategical considerations are mooted. Nothing is absolute; it is clear that many concessions must be made to necessity. But these concessions need not go too far. Otherwise the whole world would claim its military conveniences; and there would be war without end. No, it is no more the land than the race that makes a nation. The land provides the *substratum*, the field of battle and work; man provides the soul. Man is everything in the formation of that sacred thing which we call a people. Nothing of a material nature suffices for it. A nation is a spiritual principle, the result of profound historical complications, a spiritual family, not a group determined by the configuration of the soil. We have now seen what do not suffice for the creation of such a spiritual principle; race, language, interests, religious affinity, geography, military necessities. What more, then, is necessary?

III.

A nation is a living soul, a spiritual principle. Two things, which in truth are but one, constitute this soul, this spiritual principle. One is in the past, the other in the present. One is the common possession of a rich heritage of memories; the other is the actual consent, the desire to live together, the will to preserve worthily the undivided inheritance which has been handed down. Man does not improvise. The nation, like the individual, is the outcome of a long past of efforts, and sacrifices, and devotion. Ancestor-worship is therefore all the more legitimate; for our ancestors have made us what we are. A heroic past, great men, glory,—I mean glory of the genuine kind,—these form the social capital, upon which a national idea may be founded. To have common glories in the past, a common will in the present; to have done great things together, to will to do the like again,—such are the essential conditions for the making of a people. We love in proportion to the sacrifices we have consented to make, to the sufferings we have endured. We love the house that we have built, and will hand down to our descendants. The Spartan hymn, "We are what you were; we shall be what you are," is in its simplicity the national anthem of every land.

In the past an inheritance of glory and regrets to be shared, in the future a like ideal to be realised; to have suffered, and rejoiced, and hoped together; all these things are worth more than custom-houses in common, and frontiers in accordance with strategical ideas; all these can be understood in spite of diversities of race and language. I said just now, "to have suffered together," for indeed suffering in common is a greater bond of union than joy. As regards national memories, mournings are worth more than triumphs; for they impose duties, they demand common effort.

A nation is then a great solidarity, constituted by the sentiment of the sacrifices that its citizens have made, and of those that they feel prepared to make once more. It implies a past; but it is summed up in the present by a tangible fact—consent, the clearly expressed desire to live a common life. A nation's existence is—if you will pardon the metaphor—a daily plebiscite, as the individual's existence is a perpetual affirmation of life. I know very well that this is less metaphysical than divine right, less brutal than pseudo-historic right. In the order of ideas that I submit to you, a nation has no more right than a king to say to a province, "Thou art mine; I take thee unto myself." For us, a province means its inhabitants; and if any one has a right to be consulted in such an affair, it is the inhabitants. A nation never favours its true interests when it annexes or retains a country, regardless of the latter's wishes. The will of nations is then the only legitimate criterion; and to it we must always return.

We have banished from politics metaphysical and theological abstractions. What still remains? There remains man, his desires and his needs. Dismemberment, you will tell me, and, in the long run, natural decay, are the consequences of a system that puts those old organisms at the mercy of wills that are often little enlightened. It is clear that, in such a matter, no principle ought to be pushed to excess. Truths of this order are only applicable when taken as a whole, and in a very general way. Human wills change, but is there here on earth anything changeless? The nations are not something eternal. They have had their beginnings, they shall have their end. A European confederation will probably take their place. But such is not the law of the age in which we live. At the present hour, the existence of nations is good, even necessary. Their existence is the guarantee of liberty, which would be lost if the world had but one law and one master.

By their diverse and often antagonistic faculties, the nations take part in the common work of civilisation; each brings a note to that great chorus of humanity, which in sum is the highest ideal reality to which we attain. Isolated, their parts are feeble. I often tell myself that an individual who should have the faults regarded by nations as good qualities, who should feed himself with vain glory, who should be in the same way jealous, egoistical, and quarrelsome, who should be able to bear nothing without drawing the sword, would be the most unsupportable of men. But all these discords of detail disappear in the mass. Poor humanity, how much thou hast suffered! How many trials await thee still! May the spirit of wisdom be thy guide, and preserve thee from the countless perils with which thy path is sown!

But to resume: man is neither enslaved by his race, nor by his language, nor by his religion, nor by the course of rivers, nor by the direction of mountain ranges. A great aggregation of men, sane of mind, and warm of heart, creates a moral consciousness, which is called a nation. So far as this moral consciousness proves its strength, through the sacrifices exacted by the individual's abdication for the good of the community, it is legitimate and has a right to exist. If doubts arise concerning frontiers, consult the populations in dispute. They have a very good right to have a voice in the matter. This no doubt will bring a smile to the transcendentalists of politics, those infallible beings who pass their lives in self-deception, and from the height of their superior principles look down in pity upon our modest views. "Consult the populations, indeed! What artlessness! These are the pitiful French ideas, which would replace diplomacy and war by an infantine simplicity." Let us wait; let us suffer the reign of the transcendentalists to pass away; let us know how to submit to the disdain of the strong. It may be that after much unfruitful groping the world will return to our modest empirical solutions. At certain times, the way to be right in the future consists in knowing how to resign ourselves to being out of the fashion in the present.

ISLAMISM AND SCIENCE.[1]

I HAVE already so frequently proved the indulgent attention of this audience, that I ventured to choose for my subject to-day a question of the most subtle nature, full of these delicate distinctions into which it is necessary to enter resolutely, when we wish to make history leave the domain of inexactitude. The causes of historical error are nearly always to be found in a failure of precision in the use of words denoting nations and races. We speak of the Greeks, of the Romans, of the Arabs, as though these words designated human groups ever identical with themselves, without taking into account the changes due to military, religious, and linguistic conquests, to fashion, and to the great currents of every description which traverse the history of humanity. Reality does not govern itself in accordance with such simple categories. We French, for instance, are Roman by language, Greek by civilisation, and Jewish by religion. The matter of race, of capital importance in the beginning, has a constant tendency to lose that importance, when the great universal facts, known as Greek civilisation, Roman conquest, Teutonic conquest, Christianity, Islamism, the Renaissance, philosophy, and revolution pass, like grinding mill-stones, over the primitive varieties of the human family, and force them to mingle themselves in more or less homogeneous masses. It is my

[1] Lecture delivered at the Sorbonne, March 29th, 1883.

desire to unravel with you one of the greatest confusions of ideas made in this respect—that is to say, the equivocation contained in these expressions: Arabic science, Arabic philosophy, Arabic art, Mohammedan science, Mohammedan civilisation. From the vague ideas current on this matter result many false judgments, and even practical errors that are, at times, of some gravity.

Every person, however slightly he may be acquainted with the affairs of our time, sees clearly the actual inferiority of Mohammedan countries, the decadence of states governed by Islam, and the intellectual nullity of the races that hold, from that religion alone, their culture and their education. All those who have been in the East, or in Africa, are struck by the way in which the mind of a true believer is fatally limited, by the species of iron circle that surrounds his head, rendering it absolutely closed to knowledge, incapable of either learning anything, or of being open to any new idea. From his religious initiation at the age of ten or twelve years, the Mohammedan child, who occasionally may be, up to that time, of some intelligence, at a blow becomes a fanatic, full of a stupid pride in the possession of what he believes to be the absolute truth, happy as with a privilege, with what makes his inferiority. This foolish pride is the radical vice of the Mussulman. The apparent simplicity of his creed inspires him with an unjustifiable contempt for other religions. Persuaded that God gives fortune and power at his good pleasure, without taking account either of education or personal merit, the Mussulman has the most profound disdain for instruction, for science, for everything that constitutes the European spirit. This bent of mind inculcated by the Mohammedan faith is so strong, that all differences of race and nationality disappear by the fact of conversion to Islam.

The Berber, the Sudanese, the Circassian, the Malay, the Egyptian, and the Nubian, once they have become Mussulmans, are no longer Berbers, Sudanese, Egyptians, etc.; they are simply Mussulmans. To this Persia is the only exception; she has been able to keep her own genius, for Persia has known how to take a place by herself in Islam. At bottom she is more Shîite than Moslem.

To diminish the inferences hostile to Islam, which one is compelled to draw from this generally observed state of things, many persons point out that this decadence, after all, can only be a transitory phase. To reassure themselves for the future, they make appeal to the past. This Mohammedan civilisation, now so debased, was once very brilliant. It had men of science and philosophers. It was for centuries the mistress of the Christian West. Why should that which has been, not be once more? That is the precise point which I wish to discuss. Was there really a Mohammedan science, or at least a science recognised by Islam, tolerated by Islam?

There is undoubtedly in the facts alleged a partial truth. Yes; from about the year 775 to nearly the middle of the thirteenth century, that is to say, for about five hundred years, there were in Mohammedan countries learned men, thinkers of very high distinction. It might almost be said that, during this period, the Mohammedan world was superior in intellectual culture to the Christian world. But this fact must be carefully analysed, if we are to avoid drawing from it erroneous conclusions. We must follow, century by century, the history of Eastern civilisation, in order to appreciate, at their true value, the diverse elements which brought about this momentary superiority, so soon transformed into a distinct inferiority. There is nothing more alien to all that can be called philosophy or science, than the first century of Islam. The result of a religious warfare which lasted for several centuries, and held the conscience of Arabia in suspense between the different forms of Semitic monotheism, Islam is a thousand leagues from all that can be called rationalism or science. The Arab cavaliers who espoused its cause, as a pretext for conquest and pillage, were, in their time, the finest warriors in the world; but they were assuredly the least philosophical of men. An Oriental writer of the thirteenth century, Aboul-Faradj, tracing the character of the Arabian people, thus expresses himself: "The science of this people, that which gave it glory, was the science of language, the knowledge of its idioms, the texture of verse, the skilful composition of prose. As for philosophy, God had taught them none, and had not fitted them for it." Nothing can be truer. The nomad Arab, the most literary of men, is of all men the least mystical, the least inclined to meditation. The religious Arab contents himself, for the explanation of things, with a creative God, governing the world directly, and revealing himself to man by successive prophets. Thus, so long as Islam was in the hands of the Arab race, that is to say, under the first four Caliphs and under the Omeyyades, there was born within it no intellectual movement of a profane character. Omar did not burn—as we are often told—the library of Alexandria; that library had, by his time, nearly disappeared. But the principle which he caused to triumph in the world was, in a very real sense, destructive of learned research and of the varied work of the mind.

All underwent a change when, towards the year 750, Persia took the upper hand, and made the dynasty of the children of Abbas victorious over that of the Beni-Omeya. The centre of Islam found itself transported into the region of the Tigris and Euphrates. But this country was still full of the traces of one of the most brilliant civilisations that the East has ever known, that of the Persian Sassanidæ, which had reached its highest point under the rule of Chosroes Nuschirvan. For centuries past art and industry had flourished in these lands. Chosroes added intellectual activity. Philosophy, banished from Constantinople, came to Persia for refuge. Chosroes had translations made of the books of India. The Nestorian Christians, who formed the most considerable element of the population, were versed in Greek science and philosophy; medicine was entirely in their hands. Their bishops were logicians and geometricians. In the Persian epics, of which the local colour is borrowed from Sassanian times, when Rustem desires to construct a bridge, he summons to his aid a *djathalik* (*Catholicos*, the name of the Nestorian patriarchs or bishops), in the capacity of engineer.

The terrible blast of Islam completely checked, for the space of a century, all this fine Iranian development. But the advent of the Abbasides seemed like a revival of the brilliancy of the Chosroes. The revolution that gave the throne to this dynasty was brought about by Persian troops under Persian leaders. Its founders, Aboul Abbas, and, above all, Mansour, were always surrounded by Persians. These were in some measure the Sassanians resuscitated. The privy councillors, the preceptors of the princes, and the prime ministers were the Barmecides, a highly enlightened family of ancient Persia, which had remained faithful to the old Persian religion, to Parsiism, and had been tardily, and without conviction, converted to Islam. The Nestorians soon surrounded those somewhat sceptical Caliphs, and became, by a kind of exclusive privilege, their chief physicians. Harran, a town which, in the history of the human mind, has taken a place by itself, had remained Pagan; and had retained the whole scientific tradition of Greek antiquity. To the new school it furnished a large contingent of learned men, indifferent to revealed religion; and including, above all, skilful astronomers.

Bagdad arose as the capital of this renascent Persia. Arabic, the language of the conquest, could not be supplanted, nor its religion be disowned; but the spirit of the new civilisation was essentially a mingled one. Parsis and Christians took the leading part; the administration, the police in particular, was in the hands of the latter. All those brilliant caliphs, the contemporaries of our Carlovingian monarchs, Mansour, Haroun al-Raschid, Mamoun, can scarcely be called Mussulmans. Externally they practise the religion of which they are the chiefs, or popes, if one can thus express one's self; but in spirit they are elsewhere. They are curious to know all things, and chiefly things exotic and Pagan; they question India, ancient Persia, above all, Greece. At times, it is true, the Moslem pietists cause strange reactions at court; at certain moments the Caliph becomes devout, and proceeds to sacrifice his infidel or free-thinking friends. Then the independent influence takes the upper hand once more; the Caliph recalls his men of science, and his boon companions; and a free life begins anew, to the great scandal of the puritanical Mussulmans.

Such is the explanation of that strange and fascinating civilisation of Bagdad, the features of which the fables of the *Thousand and One Nights* have fixed in every imagination, a curious medley of official rigour and private relaxation, an age of youth and inconsequence, in which the serious arts and the arts of the life of pleasure flourished, thanks to the protection of the hostile chiefs of a fanatical religion; in which the libertine, though always under the menace of the most cruel punishments, was flattered and a favourite at court. Under the rule of those Caliphs, now tolerant, now reluctant persecutors, free thought developed; the *Motecallemîn* or "disputants" held debates, where all religions were examined in the light of reason. In some measure we have an account of one of those debates given by a highly devout person. Allow me to read it to you, as M. Dozy has translated it.

A doctor in Kairwan asks a pious Spanish theologian, who has journeyed to Bagdad, whether, during his stay in that town, he has ever been present at the meetings of the *Motecallemîn.* "I was twice present," replies the Spaniard; "but I shall take good care not to go again." "And why?" asks his interlocutor.

"You will judge," responds the traveller. "At the first meeting to which I went there were not only Mussulmans of every kind, orthodox and heterodox, but also unbelievers, fire-worshippers, atheists, materialists, Jews, and Christians—in fact, sceptics of every species. Each sect had its leader, whose duty it was to defend the opinions that it held; and every time one of these leaders entered the room, all rose in token of respect, and no one resumed his place until the leader was seated. The room was soon full, and, when the meeting was seen to be complete, one of the sceptics took up the discourse. 'We are gathered together for the purpose of reasoning,' he said; 'you know all the conditions. You Mussulmans will not allege reasons drawn from your Book, or based on the authority of your Prophet; for we believe in neither one nor the other. Every one must confine himself to arguments adduced from reason.'

All applauded these words. You can understand," added the Spaniard, "that after hearing such things, I returned no more to that assembly. I was induced to visit another; but it was the same scandal over again."

A genuine philosophical and scientific movement was the consequence of this momentary relaxation of orthodox rigour. The Syrian Christian physicians, successors to the later Greek schools, were well versed in the Peripatetic philosophy, in mathematics, in medicine, and in astronomy. The Caliphs employed them to translate into Arabic the Encyclopædia of Aristotle, Euclid, Galen, Ptolemy,—in a word, the whole of Greek science, as it was then known. Active minds, like that of Alkindi,[1] began to speculate on the eternal problems that man puts to himself, and is powerless to solve. They were called *Filsouf (Philosophos)*, and from that time this exotic word was taken in bad part, as designating something foreign to Islam. With the Mussulmans *Filsouf* became a name to be feared, often bringing death or persecution like *Zendik* and later still *Farmaçoun* (Free-Mason). It must be admitted that the rationalism produced in the bosom of Islam was of the most thorough character. A sort of philosophical society, which called itself the *Ikhwan es-safa*, "the brethren of sincerity," set itself to publish a philosophical encyclopædia, remarkable for its wisdom, and for the elevation of its ideas. Two very great men, Alfarabi[1] and Avicenna,[1] soon ranked with the deepest thinkers who have ever lived. Astronomy and algebra had, especially in Persia, remarkable developments. Chemistry pursued its long subterranean labours, revealing itself to the outer world by astonishing results, such as distillation and perhaps gunpowder. Moslem Spain followed the East in the pursuit of these studies; the Jews lent an

[1] See Note XI.

active collaboration. Ibn Badja,[1] Ibn Tofail,[1] and Averroes raised philosophic thought, in the twelfth century, to heights it had never reached since antiquity.

Such is that great philosophical system which we are accustomed to call Arabic, because it is written in Arabic, but which is in reality Græco-Sassanian. It would be more precise to say Greek, for the really fruitful element of all this came from Greece. One's value, in those days of abasement, was proportionate to what one knew of ancient Greece. Greece was the one source of knowledge and of exact thought. The supremacy of Greece and Bagdad over the Latin West was due to this fact alone,—that, in the former, men were much closer to the Greek tradition. It was an easier matter to have a copy of Euclid, or Ptolemy, or Aristotle, at Bagdad, or at Harran, than at Paris. If the Byzantines had only been less jealous guardians of the treasures, which at that moment they scarcely read, if in the eighth or the ninth century had lived a Bessarion[2] or a Lascaris,[2] there would have been no need for that strange detour, by which Greek science reached us in the twelfth century, after passing through Syria, Bagdad, Cordova, and Toledo. But that species of mysterious providence which causes the torch of humanity, when it begins to expire in the hands of one people, to pass into the hands of another which uplifts and lights it anew, gave a value of the highest order to the work, otherwise apt to be obscure, of those poor Syrians, of those persecuted *Filsouf*, of those Harranians, whose scepticism put them under the ban of their contemporaries. It was by those Arabic translations of Greek works of philosophy and science that Europe was plunged into the ferment of ancient tradition, needful for the birth of her genius.

[1] See Note XII. [2] See Note XIII.

In fact, while Averroes, the last of the Arabic philosophers, was dying in Morocco, in sadness and abandonment, this West of ours was fully awakening out of its slumber. Abelard had already given the cry of renascent rationalism. Europe had found her genius, and was commencing upon that extraordinary evolution, the last term of which will be the complete emancipation of the human mind. Here on the mount of St. Geneviève, a new *sensorium* was created for the work of the mind. One thing was wanting—books, the pure sources of antiquity. At a first glance, it would seem as though the more natural thing to have done would have been to go and ask for them in the libraries of Constantinople, where the originals were to be found, than to have depended upon translations, often mediocre, and in a language but ill fitted to render Greek thought. But religious controversy had created between the Latin world and the Greek world a deplorable antipathy, which the fatal crusade of 1204 only served to intensify. And then we had no Greek scholars; it was necessary to wait for three hundred years before we had a Budé,[1] a Lefèvre d'Étaples.[1]

In default of the true and authentic Greek philosophy which was in the Byzantine libraries, it was incumbent to go to Spain, and seek there a Greek science translated badly and sophisticated. I shall not speak of Gerbert,[2] about whose travels among the Mussulmans there hangs much doubt. But even in the eleventh century, Constantine the African[2] was superior in learning to his age and country, because he had received a Moslem education. From 1130 to 1150 an active college of translators, established at Toledo under the patronage of Archbishop Raymond, put into Latin the most important works of

1 See Note XIV. 2 See Note XV.

Arabic science. In the early years of the thirteenth century, the Arabic Aristotle made its triumphant entrance into the University of Paris. The West threw off its inferiority, which had lasted for four or five hundred years. Till then Europe had been, as regarded science, tributary to the Mussulmans. Towards the middle of the thirteenth century the balance was still uncertain. Starting from about the year 1275, two easily discernible movements are apparent. On the one hand, the Mohammedan countries plunge into the most pitiable intellectual decadence; on the other, Western Europe resolutely enters on its own account into that great highway of the scientific search for truth, that immense curve, the amplitude of which cannot yet be gauged.

Woe to him that becomes useless to human progress! He is almost instantly cast aside. When the so-called Arabic science had inoculated the Latin West with its germ of life, it disappeared. While Averroes was arriving in the Latin schools of thought at a celebrity almost equal to that of Aristotle himself, he was forgotten by his co-religionists. After about the year 1200 there was no longer a single Arabic philosopher of any renown. Philosophy had ever been persecuted in the bosom of Islam, but by means that had not succeeded in suppressing it. From the year 1200, the theological reaction carried it away altogether. Philosophy was abolished in Mohammedan countries. The historians and other writers only speak of it as a memory, and that an evil memory. The philosophical manuscripts were destroyed, and have become rare. Astronomy is only tolerated for the sake of that part of it which serves to determine the direction of prayer. Soon the Turkish race assumed the hegemony of Islam, and caused the universal prevalence of its total lack of the philosophic and scientific spirit. From that moment, with some rare exceptions, like Ibn Khaldoun,[1] Islam no longer counted among its members any man of great mind. It has slain the science and philosophy within itself.

I have not sought to diminish the rôle of that great science, known as Arabic, which marks such an important stage in the history of the human mind. On some points its originality has been exaggerated, notably with regard to astronomy; but we need not go to the other extreme, and depreciate it beyond measure. Between the disappearance of ancient civilisation in the sixth century, and the birth of the European genius in the twelfth and thirteenth, there was what can be called the Arabic period, during which the traditions of the human spirit were continued by the regions conquered by Islam. In reality what was Arabic in this so-called Arabic science? The language, and nothing but the language. The Moslem conquest had borne the language of the Hedjaz to the very ends of the earth. It was with Arabic as with Latin, which in the West became the vehicle of feelings and thoughts that had nothing to do with ancient Latium. Averroes, Avicenna, Albateni,[2] were Arabs, as Albertus Magnus,[3] Roger Bacon, Francis Bacon, and Spinoza were Latins. It is as great a mistake to give the credit of Arabic science and philosophy to Arabia, as to put all the Latin Christian literature, all the Scholastic Philosophy, all the Renaissance, and the whole of the science of the fifteenth, and in part of the sixteenth centuries, to the credit of the city of Rome; because all this was written in Latin. What is in fact a very remarkable thing is, that among the philosophers and learned men called Arabic, there was but one alone, Alkindi, who was of Arabic origin; all the others were Persians,

[1] See Note XVI. [2] See Note XVII. [3] See Note XVIII.

Transoxians, Spaniards, natives of Bokhara, of Samarcand, of Cordova, of Seville. Not only were those men not Arabs by blood, but they were in nowise Arabs in mind. They made use of Arabic; but they were fettered by it, as the mediæval thinkers were fettered by Latin, and modified it for their own use. Arabic, which lends itself so well to poetry, and to a certain eloquence, is a very unsuitable instrument for metaphysics. The Arabic philosophers and men of science were in general somewhat bad writers.

This science, then, is not Arabic. Is it at least Mohammedan? Has Islamism lent any tutelary aid to rational research? In no way. This splendid advance in learning was entirely the work of Parsees, of Christians, of Jews, of Harranians, of Ismaelians, of Mussulmans in internal revolt against their own religion. From orthodox Mussulmans it only reaped curses. Mamoun, the Caliph who showed most zeal for the introduction of Greek philosophy, was pitilessly damned by the theologians; the misfortunes that afflicted his reign were represented as penalties for his tolerance of doctrines alien to Islam. It was no rare circumstance for the books of philosophy and astronomy to be burnt in public places, or cast into wells and cisterns, to please the populace, aroused by the Imams. Those who cultivated these studies were called *Zendiks* (unbelievers); they were stoned in the streets, their houses were set on fire, and very frequently the authorities, when they desired to secure popularity, would put them to death.

Islamism has then, in reality, constantly persecuted science and philosophy. It ended by stifling it. It is, however, necessary to distinguish in this respect two periods in the history of Islam—one from its commencement to the twelfth century, the other from the thirteenth century to our own days. In the former period Islam, undermined by sects, and tempered by a species of protestantism (known as *Motazelism*), was much less organised and less fanatical than it has been in the latter, when it has fallen into the hands of the Tartar and Berber races—races which are heavy, brutal, and without intelligence. Islamism offers this peculiarity: that it has obtained from its disciples a faith ever tending to grow stronger. The first Arabs engaged in the movement scarcely believed in the mission of the Prophet. During two or three centuries incredulity was scarcely dissimulated. Then came the absolute reign of dogma, without any possible separation of the spiritual from the temporal, the reign of coercion and corporeal punishments for him who did not practise religion; a system, finally, which has only been exceeded, in regard to persecutions, by the Spanish Inquisition. Liberty is never more grievously wounded than by a social organisation, in which religion absolutely dominates civil life. In modern times we have seen only two examples of such a rule—on the one hand the Moslem States, on the other the former Papal State, in the days of its temporal power. And it ought to be remarked that the temporal papacy only weighed upon a country of very limited extent; while Islamism oppresses vast portions of our globe, and in them maintains the idea most opposed to progress,—the state founded on a pseudo-Revelation, theology governing society.

The liberals who defend Islam do not know its real nature. Islam is the close union of the spiritual and the temporal; it is the reign of a dogma, it is the heaviest chain that humanity has ever borne. In the first half of the Middle Ages, I repeat, Islam supported philosophy because it could not prevent it; it could not prevent it, because it was itself lacking in cohesion, and only poorly equipped against terrorism. The police was, as I have said, in the hands of the Christians; and was chiefly occupied in checking the attempts of the followers of Ali.[1] A multitude of things passed through the meshes of that loosely held net. But when Islam had at its disposal masses of ardent believers, it destroyed all. Religious terror and hypocrisy were the order of the day. Islam has been liberal in its day of weakness, and violent in its day of strength. Do not let us honour it then for what it has been unable to suppress. To do honour to Islam for the philosophy and science that it did not annihilate from the very first, is as though we were to do honour to the theologians for the discoveries of modern science. These discoveries are made in spite of the theologians. Western theology has not persecuted less than that of Islamism; only it has not been successful, it has not crushed out the modern spirit, as Islamism has trodden out the spirit of the lands it has conquered.

In our Western Europe theological persecution has only succeeded in a single country—Spain. There a terrible system of oppression has stifled the scientific spirit. Let us hasten to say that that noble land will have her revenge. In Moslem countries has come to pass what would have happened in Europe, if the Inquisition, Philip II., and Pius V. had succeeded in their design of arresting the human mind. Frankly, I have much difficulty in being grateful to people for desisting from the evil that they have been unable to achieve. No; religions have their great and beautiful hours, when they console and raise the feeble parts of our poor humanity; but we need not compliment them for what has been born in spite of them, for what they have sought to smother in the cradle. We do not

[1] See Note XIX.

inherit the possessions of the people whom we assassinate; we ought not to allow persecutors to profit from the things that they have persecuted.

That is, however, the error that we commit, by an excess of generosity, when we attribute to the influence of Islam a movement which produced itself in spite of Islam, against Islam, and which Islam has happily been unable to prevent. Doing honour to the Islam of Avicenna, of Avenzoar,[1] of Averroes, is like doing honour to the Catholicism of Galileo. Theology impeded Galileo; it was not sufficiently strong to fetter him altogether. That is no reason for his owing it any great gratitude. Far from me be it to speak, with words of bitterness, against any of the symbols in which the human conscience has sought for rest, amongst the insoluble problems presented to it by the universe and its destiny. Islamism has its beauties as a religion; I have never entered a mosque without a vivid emotion—shall I even say without a certain regret in not being a Mussulman? But to the human reason Islamism has only been injurious. The minds that it has shut from the light were, no doubt, already closed in by their own internal limits; but it has persecuted free thought, I shall not say more violently than other religions, but more effectually. It has made of the countries that it has conquered a closed field to the rational culture of the mind.

What is, in fact, essentially distinctive of the Mussulman is his hatred of science, his persuasion that research is useless, frivolous, almost impious—the natural sciences, because they are attempts at rivalry with God; the historical sciences, because, since they apply to times anterior to Islam, they may revive ancient heresies. One of the most

[1] See Note XX.

curious evidences of this is that of the Sheik Rifaa, who resided in Paris for several years, as chaplain of the Egyptian school; and after his return to Egypt wrote a work full of the quaintest observations on French society. His fixed idea is that European science, above all by its principle of the permanence of natural laws, is from one end to the other a heresy; and it must be admitted that, from the point of view of Islam, he is not altogether wrong. A revealed dogma is always opposed to the free research that may contradict it. The result of science is not to banish the divine altogether, but ever to place it at a greater distance from the world of particular facts in which men once believed they saw it. Experience causes the supernatural to draw back, and restrains its domain. But the supernatural is the basis of all theology. Islam, in treating science as an enemy, is only consistent; but it is a dangerous thing to be too consistent. To its own misfortune Islam has been successful. By slaying science it has slain itself; and is condemned in the world to a complete inferiority.

When one starts from the idea that scientific research is a thing that infringes on the rights of God, one inevitably comes to sloth of mind, to lack of precision, to incapacity for exactitude. *Allah aalam:* "God knoweth best what it is," is the last word of all Moslem discussion. It is a good thing to believe in God, but not to such an extent as that. In the early days of his sojourn at Mossoul, Sir Henry Layard desired, clear-minded as he was, to acquire some information on the population of the town, on its commerce, and on its historical traditions. He addressed himself to the Cadi, who gave the following response, the translation of which has been kindly furnished to me:—

"O my illustrious friend, O joy of living men! What

thou askest of me is both useless and harmful. Albeit all my days have been spent in this land, I have never sought to count the houses, or to inform myself of the number of their inhabitants. And as to what merchandise this man putteth upon his mules, and that man in the hold of his ship, in very truth these are things that concern me not at all. As for the former history of this city, God alone knoweth it; and He alone could say with how many errors its dwellers were filled before it was overcome by Islam. The knowledge of it would be dangerous for us.

"O my friend, O my lamb, seek not to know the things that concern thee not. Thou hast come amongst us, and we have made thee welcome; go in peace! Verily, all the words that thou hast said unto me have done me no ill; for he that speaketh is one, and he that giveth ear is another. After the manner of the men of thy nation, thou hast journeyed through many lands, but not the more hast thou found happiness anywhere. We (blessed be God!) were born here, and have no desire to go hence.

"Hearken unto me, my son; there is no wisdom like unto that of faith in God. He hath created the world; who are we that we should strive to equal Him by seeking to fathom the mysteries of His creation? Behold that star that goeth round another star; behold yet another star that draweth a tail behind it, and is so many years in coming, and so many years in departing. Leave it, my son; He whose hands have fashioned it, knoweth well how to lead and direct it.

"But it may be that thou shalt say: 'O man, get thee gone; for I am wiser than thou, and have looked upon things whereof thou knowest not.' If thou thinkest that these things have made thee better than I, be doubly welcome; but as for me, I bless God that I have not sought after that of which I have no need. Thou art learned in things that have no interest for me; and what thou hast seen, I disdain. Shall greater knowledge give thee a second belly, and shall thine eyes, that go prying everywhere, make thee find a Paradise?

"O my friend, if it be that thou hast a desire to be happy, let this be thy cry, 'God alone is God!' Do no evil, and then thou shalt fear neither men nor death itself, for thine hour shall come."

This Cadi is very philosophical after his own fashion; but note the difference. We consider the Cadi's letter charming; but he, on the contrary, would deem what we are saying here to be abominable. Besides, it is for society that the consequences of such a way of thinking are fatal. Of the two evils that follow in the train of lack of the scientific spirit, superstition and dogmatism, the latter is perhaps worse than the former. The East is not superstitious; its great evil is the narrow dogmatism imposed by the whole force of society. The goal of humanity is not repose in a resigned ignorance; it is an implacable war with falsehood, a struggle with the powers of darkness.

Science is the very soul of a society; for science is reason. It creates military superiority and industrial superiority. Some day it will create social superiority—that is to say, a state of society in which the amount of justice compatible with the essence of the universe will be attained. Science gives force for the service of reason. In Asia there are elements of barbarism analogous to those that formed the early Moslem armies, and the great cyclones of Attila and Genghis Khan. But science bars their way. If Omar or Genghis Khan had found good artillery confronting them, they would never have passed the borders of their desert. We need not stop at momentary aberrations.

What was not said at the beginning against fire-arms, which nevertheless have contributed much to the victory of civilisation? For my own part, I am convinced that science is good, that it alone can furnish weapons against the evil that can be wrought by it; and that in the end it will only serve progress;—I mean true progress—that which is inseparable from respect for humanity and freedom.

Appendix to the preceding Lecture.

(A remarkably intelligent Afghan sheik, visiting Paris, having published in the *Journal des Débats* of May 18th, 1883, some remarks upon the preceding lecture, I replied next day in the same journal, as follows.—*Author's Note.*)

The very judicious reflections which my last lecture at the Sorbonne suggested to Sheik Gemmal Eddin were read yesterday with the interest which they deserved. There is nothing more instructive than thus to study, in its original and sincere manifestations, the conscience of the enlightened Asiatic. It is by listening to the most diverse voices, coming from the four quarters of the horizon in favour of rationalism, that one comes to the conclusion that if religion divides men, reason tends to unite them; and that, at bottom, there is but one reason. The unity of the human mind is the great and consoling consequence which results from the peaceful encounter of ideas, when the antagonistic pretensions of so-called supernatural revelations are put on one side. The league of the whole world's honest thinkers against fanaticism and superstition is apparently composed of an imperceptible minority; essentially it is the only league destined to endure, for it rests upon truth, and will end by winning the day, after the fables that rival it have been exhausted in lengthened series of powerless convulsions.

Nearly two months ago I made the acquaintance of the Sheik Gemmal Eddin, thanks to my dear colleague, M. Ganem. Few persons have produced a more vivid impression upon me. It was in great measure my conversation with him that decided me in choosing for the subject of my lecture at the Sorbonne the relation between the scientific spirit and Islamism. The Sheik Gemmal Eddin is an Afghan, entirely emancipated from the prejudices of Islam; he belongs to those energetic races of the Upper Iran bordering upon India, in which the Aryan spirit still flourishes so strongly, under the superficial garb of official Islamism. He is the best proof of that great axiom, which we have often proclaimed, that the worth of religions is to be determined by the worth of the races that profess them. The freedom of his thought, his noble and loyal character, made me believe, when in his presence, that I had before me, in a resuscitated state, one of my old acquaintances, Avicenna, Averroes, or some other of those great sceptics who for five centuries represented the tradition of the human spirit. The contrast was especially apparent to me when I compared this striking similarity with the spectacle presented by Moslem countries other than Persia, countries where scientific and philosophical curiosity is so rare a thing. The Sheik Gemmal Eddin is the finest case of racial protest against religious conquest that could be cited. He confirms what the intelligent orientalists of Europe have frequently said, namely, that Afghanistan is in all Asia, Japan alone excepted, the country which presents most of the constituent elements of that which we call a nation.

In the Sheik's learned article I can only see a single point on which we really differ. The Sheik does not admit the distinctions, which historical criticism leads us to make, in these great and complex facts called empires and conquests. The Roman Empire, with which the Arabic conquest has so much in common, made the Latin language the organ of the human spirit through the whole of the Western world up to the sixteenth century. Albertus Magnus, Roger Bacon, and Spinoza wrote in Latin. They are not however, for us, Latins. In a history of English literature we assign a place to Bede and Alcuin, in a history of French literature we place Gregory of Tours and Abelard. It is not that we think lightly of the action of Rome in the history of civilisation, any more than we fail to recognise Arabic action. But these great currents of humanity demand analysis. All that is written in Latin is not to the glory of Rome; all that is written in Greek is not Hellenic work; all that is written in Arabic is not of Arabic production; all that is done in a Christian country is not the result of Christianity; all that is done in a Mohammedan country is not the fruit of Islam. This is the principle which the profound historian of Moslem Spain, M. Reinhard Dozy, whose loss learned Europe is at this moment deploring, applied with so rare a sagacity. These sorts of distinctions are necessary, if we do not wish history to be a tissue of inexactitude and misunderstanding.

One aspect in which I have appeared unjust to the Sheik, is that I have not sufficiently developed the idea that all revealed religion is forced to show hostility to positive science; and that, in this respect, Christianity has no reason to boast over Islam. About that there can be no doubt. Galileo was not treated more kindly by

Catholicism than was Averroes by Islam. Galileo found truth in a Catholic country despite Catholicism, as Averroes nobly philosophised in a Moslem country despite Islam. If I did not insist more strongly upon this point, it was, to tell the truth, because my opinions on this matter are so well known that there was no need for me to recur to them again before a public conversant with my writings. I have said, sufficiently often to preclude any necessity for repeating it, that the human mind must be detached from all supernatural belief if it desires to labour at its own essential task, which is the construction of positive science. This does not imply any violent destruction or hasty rupture. It does not mean that the Christian should forsake Christianity, or that the Mussulman should abandon Islam. It means that the enlightened parts of Christendom and Islam should arrive at that state of benevolent indifference in which religious beliefs become inoffensive. This is half accomplished in nearly all Christian countries. Let us hope that the like will be the case for Islam. Naturally on that day the Sheik and I will be at one, and ready to applaud heartily.

I did not assert that all Mussulmans, without distinction of race, are, and always will be, sunk in ignorance: I said that Islamism puts great difficulties in the way of science, and unfortunately has succeeded for five or six hundred years in almost suppressing it in the countries under its sway; and that this is for these countries a cause of extreme weakness. I believe, in point of fact, that the regeneration of the Mohammedan countries will not be the work of Islam; it will come to pass through the enfeeblement of Islam, as indeed the great advance of the countries called Christian commenced with the destruction of the tyrannical church of the Middle Ages. Some persons have seen in my lecture a thought hostile to the individuals who profess the Mohammedan religion. That is by no means true; Mussulmans are themselves the first victims of Islam. More than once in my Eastern travels I have been in a position to notice how fanaticism proceeds from a small number of dangerous men who keep the others in the practice of religion by terror. To emancipate the Mussulman from his religion would be the greatest service that one could render him. In wishing these populations, in which so many good elements exist, a deliverance from the yoke that weighs them down, I do not believe that I have any unkindly thought for them. And, let me say also, since the Sheik Gemmal Eddin desires me to hold the balance equally between different faiths, I should not any the more believe that I was wishing evil of certain European countries if I expressed a hope that Christianity should have a less dominant influence upon them.

The lack of agreement between liberal thinkers on these different points is not very serious, since, favourable or not to Islam, all come to the same practical conclusion, the necessity for spreading education among Mohammedans. This is perfectly right, if by education is meant serious education of a character to cultivate the reason. If the religious leaders of Islamism contribute to this excellent work I shall be delighted. To be frank, I am a little doubtful of their doing so. Distinguished individualities—there will be few so distinguished as the Sheik Gemmal Eddin—will be formed who will sever their connection with Islam as we ourselves have separated from Catholicism. Certain countries in time will almost break with the religion of the Koran; but I suspect that the movement of Renaissance will be made without the support of official Islam. The scientific Renaissance of Europe was to no greater extent carried on with the assistance of Catholicism; at the present hour—and we have no reason to be surprised at it—Catholicism still struggles to prevent the full realisation of that which sums up the rational cloud of humanity, the neutral state outside so-called revealed dogmas.

Above all else, as a supreme law, let us put freedom and respect for men. Not to destroy religions, even to treat them with kindliness as free manifestations of human nature, but not to guarantee them, most of all not to defend them against such of their own members as desire to leave them,—this is the duty of civil society. Thus reduced to the condition of free and independent studies, like literature or taste, religions will be entirely transformed. Deprived of the official or temporal bond, they will disintegrate and lose the greater part of their drawbacks. All this is Utopian at the present hour; all this will be reality in the future. How will each religion comport itself under the reign of liberty, which, after many actions and reactions, is destined to impose itself upon human societies? It is not in a few lines that such a problem can be examined. In my lecture I merely wished to treat an historical question. The Sheik Gemmal Eddin seems to me to have brought considerable arguments in support of my two fundamental theses: During the first half of its existence Islam did not prevent the scientific movement from growing in Mohammedan soil; during the second half of its existence it stifled the scientific movement within it, and that to its own misfortune.

FAREWELL TO TOURGENIEF.[1]

Not without a word of farewell shall we allow the bier to depart, which is to give back to his own country the guest of genius, whom through long years it has been our privilege to know and to love. A master in the art of judging the things of the imagination will tell you the secret of those exquisite works which have charmed our century. Tourguenief was a great writer; above all else, he was a great man. I shall only speak to you of his personality, as it has appeared to me in the sweet seclusion among us which an illustrious friendship had conferred upon him.

From the mysterious decree which prescribes the vocations of men, Tourguenief received the noblest gift of all: he was born essentially impersonal. His mind was not that of an individual more or less richly endowed by nature; it was in some measure the mind of a people. Before his birth he had lived thousands of years; infinite series of dreams concentrated themselves in the depths of his heart. No other man has been to such a point the incarnation of a whole race. A world lived in him, spoke through his lips; generations of ancestors, lost and speechless in the slumber of the ages, found in him life and utterance.

The silent spirit of collective masses is the source of all great things. But the mass has no voice. It can only feel

[1] Spoken at the *Gare du Nord*, October 1st, 1883.

and stammer. It must have an interpreter, a prophet who may speak for it. What manner of man shall this prophet be? Who shall tell of those sufferings, denied by those whose interest it is not to behold them, those secret longings that derange the beatific optimism of the satisfied? The great man, when he is at the same time a man of genius, is a man of feeling. That is why the great man is of all men the least free. He does not do, he does not say, what he wills. A God speaks in him; ten centuries of sorrow and hope possess and command him. At times it happens to him, as to the seer in the old Biblical narrative, that being called to curse, he blesses; his tongue obeys not himself, but the Spirit that breathes upon it.

The honour of that great Slavonic race, whose appearance on the world's stage is the most unexpected phenomenon of our time, is that it has been at the very outset depicted by such an accomplished master. Never were the mysteries of an obscure, and as yet contradictory consciousness, revealed with so marvellous an insight. It was so, because Tourguenief at once felt, and saw himself feel, was at once a part of the people and one of the elect. He was as sensitive as a woman, and as impassible as an anatomist; as disillusioned as a philosopher, and as tender as a child. Happy the race which, at its entrance into reflective life, could be represented by such creations, as naïve as they are profound, at once realistic and mystical! When the future has given us the full measure of the surprises that this extraordinary Slavonic genius has in store for us, with its fiery faith, its profundity of intuition, its peculiar ideas of life and death, its need for martyrdom, its thirst for the ideal, Tourguenief's pictures will be priceless documents, in some measure like the portrait of a man of genius in his childhood, if we could but have it. Tourguenief saw the perilous gravity of his position, as interpreter of one of the great families of humanity. He felt that he had the charge of souls; and because he was an honest man, he weighed his every word, he trembled for what he said, and for what he left unsaid.

His mission was thus one of pacification. He was like the God in the Book of Job, who "maketh peace upon the high places." What in others was the cause of discord, became in him the principle of harmony. In his ample breast contradictions were reconciled, anathema and hate were disarmed by the magic spell of his art. That is why he is the common glory of schools between which exist so many diversities of opinion. A great race divided by very reason of its greatness, in him finds its unity once more. Brothers at variance, separated by diverse fashions of conceiving the ideal, come one and all to his tomb; all of you have the right to love him, for to all of you he belonged; he held all of you in his heart. What an admirable privilege is that of the man of genius! For him the repulsive sides of things have no existence. In him all is reconciled; the parties most sharply opposed to each other unite to praise and admire him. In the region to which he transports us, words, irritant to the vulgar, lose their venom. Genius does in a day the work of centuries. It creates a higher atmosphere of peace, where those that were adversaries find that in reality they have been collaborators; it opens the era of the great amnesty, when those who have fought in the arena of progress sleep side by side and hand in hand.

Above the race, in fact, there is humanity, or, if you will, reason. Tourguenief was of a race by his manner of feeling and portraying; he belongs to humanity at large by a high philosophy, that views with unflinching vision the conditions of human existence, and without prejudice seeks the knowledge of reality. This philosophy led him to tenderness, to joy of life, to pity for his fellow-creatures,—above all, for the oppressed. He had an ardent love for our poor humanity, assuredly often blind, but as often betrayed by its leaders. He applauded its spontaneous movement after truth and righteousness. He did not wish to feast on its illusions; he had no desire to complain of them. The iron temperament that mocks at those that suffer, was not his. No deception barred his path. Like the universe, he a thousand times recommenced the unachieved work; he knew well that justice can afford to wait, that in the end all will return to it. In truth, he had the words of eternal life, the words of peace, of justice, of love, and of liberty.

Farewell, then, great and dear friend. What is to journey far from us is but dust. What in you was deathless, your spiritual image, will abide with us. May your bier be, for those that come to kiss it, a gage of love in a single faith in liberal progress. And when you repose in your country's earth, may all those that repair to your tomb have a touch of sympathetic memory for the distant land where you found so many hearts to understand and to love you.

THE DEITY OF THE BOURGEOIS

(THE THEOLOGY OF BÉRANGER).

A TITLE attracted my attention lately amongst announcements of new books—*Le Béranger des Familles* (Paris: Perotin, 1859). I was curious to see how M. Béranger had been reconciled with religion and morality, and at the price of what sacrifices one can become in France the evening reading of virtuously thinking families. Examination has proved to me, that the operation which transfigures those whom popular legend has already consecrated can be performed with a very light hand, and that, if there are sins that France does not pardon, there are also others which she covers with a very easy absolution. I naïvely supposed that the new editor's preface would include some explanation of the literary singularity of a poet who has sung of everything save religion and the domestic virtues, becoming a classical author for educational seminaries, in an age so easy to scandalise as our own. There is nothing of the kind. I am only informed that: "Although he may have enjoyed his youth so long as he was young, he was before all else a good man; . . . that he is not only a great poet, but the patriarch of the new France, and that he has bequeathed to us, along with his verse, the example of his character and the lesson of his virtues." Heaven forbid that I should personify France in M. Béranger! France is essentially the land of varied and contrary gifts; and one is ever deceived when one attempts to assign limits to her nature. But almost indisputable authority has proclaimed Béranger to be the "national poet"; and the opinion expressed in the preface just cited tends more and more to become general and almost official. One is consequently justified in reflecting upon this curious adoption, and in attempting to discover on what side of the French genius its accomplishment was possible.

I have only read M. Béranger very lately, and have read his works as one would read an historical document. I am not, therefore, in a good position to understand him well; and I suspect myself of a certain injustice in the feelings which inspire me. His language, which seems to me wanting in limpidity and true lightness of touch, has perhaps a better effect when it is sung. Several of his poetical motives, which for us are meaningless, doubtless once had a significance, since they were greeted with so much favour. A perpetual misconception, to which, it appears to me, the public has not been very sensitive, also spoils for me his most successful lyrics, and mingles itself like a dissonance with his harmonious rhythms. I refer to that affectation which so often made him pay tribute to one of the faults of our age—the mania for confusing styles, and turning everything into declamation. Each style is good, provided it be free and forcible. Our old song-writers of the Provençal school are classics in their way. Anacreon sang of pleasure in a manner that was almost a lesson in morals, since it was a lesson in simplicity, grace, and good taste. Hafiz[1] is above all an incomparable debauchee. The profound melancholy of human conditions, the instability of fortune, the fatality which presses upon us, never had a more profound interpreter. The thought of death is his

[1] See Note XXI.

boon companion; behind pleasure there lies hidden for him, not vulgar gaiety but rest in the infinite, the vision of God. Everything that is true must have its place in æsthetics. The bad is that which is artificial; it is the honest and pedantic Chapelain clumsily usurping the part of bard and *trouvère;* it is the eighteenth century poet, a J. B. Rousseau or a Piron writing at will pious canticles, Pindaric odes, and obscene epigrams; it is the respectable song-writer conscientiously singing of wine, and "celebrating the favours of Glycera," as the compulsory theme for everybody who wishes to write in verse.

Certainly it would be unjust to place M. Béranger in this class of artificial and worthless writers. But it cannot be denied that his work fails to remove from the critic's eyes a singular difficulty. He was, it is said, a sober man of rare judgment, full of good counsels, little given to drinking, and much more prudent than he would have his songs make us believe. When I learnt all this I was almost tempted to cry out, "So much the worse." Had he been a rake, I should have placed him beside his brothers, the representatives of ancient gaiety, who were not in the habit of making social and philosophical songs, and saw nothing beyond their joyous refrains. But if I am told that Lisette and the burgundy are rhetorical figures, that the careless singer who pretends to have no other needs than dinners at the *Caveau*[1] and his mistress, has a philosophy, a system of politics, and (Heaven pardon me!) a theology, all my æsthetic theories are put to confusion. I no longer see anything more in the expression of this sham gaiety than a school-boy's exercise in composition, something analogous to the Latin verses which, in the days of the Roman Empire, the more cultured man used to make

[1] See Note XXII.

as a poetic system and in token of his admiration for Horace. Is it in truth conceivable that, in a century preoccupied with problems as serious as those which press upon us, a man of sense should have accepted before the public this rôle of sham drunkard and sham libertine? How can a man calmly choose a form of literature in which the essential condition of remaining truthful is to be a bad character? Désaugiers, inferior as he is to Béranger in what might be called range of intellect, seems to me a far better lyrist; for he has no underlying meaning. His gaiety is quite the old inconsequent gaiety; even had he wished it, he could have made nothing but songs. But M. Béranger wrote epics; in his day he was the solemn poet of a political school. Everything exhibits him to us as a very shrewd man with a rather narrow but clear-sighted intellect. His modesty is then feigned, and in fact he himself, at the end of his days, forsook his conventional poetics to seek for popularity in the philanthropical song and sentimental socialism.

Art and poetry are not morality. They are not the opposite of it, as some critics think; art and poetry, in a sense, suppose morality. But it would be impossible for us to say that the end of the artist and the poet is the same as that of the moralist. Aristophanes and Shakespeare often present us with the ugliest side of human nature in all its nakedness, without, on that account, any one after having read their writings finding himself humiliated or perverted. Lord Byron's Sardanapalus is noble even in his debauchery; the picture of the life of the Borgias in Burchard's narratives has the beauty of a tempest or an abyss. But pert vice, flirtation with immorality, the prettiness of evil,—there we have the French vice *par excellence*, the meanness, the folly from which the Frenchman fancies he cleanses himself by his easy air and his eternal smile. And there, too, we have that of which great poetry will never be made. There is no poetry of loose morals. Take the man of genius in his moments of aberration, a Schiller at the outset of his career for example, and you will see that it is the intoxication of some beautiful principle wrongly applied that leads him astray, not the taste of the rakehell, or the rodomontade of levity. The day on which Beaumarchais was applauded after Molière was the day on which the *bourgeoisie* (I use this word in an intellectual and not a social sense) took possession of the pit, and, installing themselves therein, hounded genius and high art from the stage.

Of all the parts of Béranger's poetical system that which surprised me most, when I read him for the first time, was his theology. I was then little versed in knowledge of the French intellect; I did not know the singular alternations of levity and dulness, of narrow timidity and foolish temerity, which are among the features of its character. All my ideas were upset when I saw how this joyous boon companion, whom I had figured to myself as a thorough-going infidel, speaking of the Almighty in highly-finished terms, and inviting his mistress to

> "Lever les yeux vers ce monde invisible
> Où pour toujours nous nous réunissons."

The song-writer of old had no theology about him; he was an atheist by essence. Not that he denied the Deity; that would have been a speculative effort of which the inoffensive creature was quite incapable; but, bound up as he was in his good and patriarchal jollity, his whole religion consisted in doing no harm to anybody. The song of the deist was then unheard in the land.

The Philistine simplicity of this new-fashioned theology,

and this custom of inclining one's self, glass in hand, before the God whom I sought with trembling, were for me a flash of light. To the indignation which the idea of religious brotherhood with those who worshipped in this way caused me, was added an impression of the fatal limitation of manners of seeing and feeling in France. The incurable religious mediocrity of this great country, orthodox even in its merry-making, was revealed to me, and the God of good folk appeared to me as the eternal *Gaulois* deity, against whom philosophy and enlightened religion, with all their endeavours, would struggle in vain.

Since then, when I have sought to account to myself for the way in which this circumstance scandalised me, I have discovered that there is nothing so relative as our judgments on levity and its opposite when intellectual matters are in question. A year, a revolution, a degree of latitude, in this respect bring about curious changes. This scoffer, whom everybody once thought so delightful, now appears to us to be closed to all the finer shades of feeling. On the one hand, we are wounded by his laughter: when he holds up to mockery the holy oil and Notre Dame de Liesse, he offends us; for think how many simple hearts have quickened at the sight of these towers, at hearing of those miracles. On the other hand, his god of *grisettes* and topers, this god in whom one can believe without being pure in habits or lofty in soul, seems to us like the Bœotian myth substituted for that of the ancient faith. We are tempted to become atheists to escape his deism, and devotees to avoid being the accomplices of his vapidity. So far is this the case that (such has been the path followed by the religious spirit in a quarter of a century) the orthodox singer of 1828 now appears to us as at once a blasphemer and a Philistine.

True religion, in fact, is the fruit of silence and meditation. It is synonymous with distinction, loftiness of spirit, and refinement; it is born with moral delicacy at the moment when the virtuous man, communing within himself, listens to the voices that are there mingled. In that silence, when every sense is lulled to quiet, when every sound from the outside world is hushed, a sweet and penetrating murmur comes from the soul, and, like the distant pealing of village bells, brings back the mystery of the infinite. Then, like a lost child who vainly seeks to unravel the secret of his unknown birth, the meditative man feels that he is in a strange and alien land. A thousand signs recall his own true homeland, and mournfully he returns there. Above the miry domain of reality he mounts to fields flooded with the light of the sun; in his nostrils are those perfumes of ancient days that the southern seas still breathed forth, when Alexander's ships fared first across their waters. Death, in the garb of a pilgrim returning from the Holy Land, knocks at the door of the soul, and the soul begins to feel what it knew not in the turmoil of life,—the sweetness of dying. Then is it assured that its works shall follow it; truth appears as the recompense of the good deeds that it has wrought. It sees how ill all transient forms suffice to express the ideal; the words "being" and "not being" lose their contradictory sense; it envisages itself in kinship with the Divine, as a son with his father, and in such utterance it prays, "Our Father which art in heaven. . . ."

What right has the dissipated man to these fugitive impressions? Is not the superficial spirit that does not see the divine sense of life, the atheist *par excellence?* Man is religious at the moment when the feeling of the infinite triumphs within him over caprice or passion. I understand

Horace's fine irony in relegating as far as possible from him the gods of whom he has no need. *Namque deos didici securum agere ævum.* I understand M. Alfred de Musset's religion, at times somewhat fantastical, but never vulgar. His joy is not gaiety; when he would fain laugh he constrains himself. But then it is the true God that he worships.

> " Je ne puis; malgré moi l'infini me tourmente.
> Je n'y saurais songer sans crainte et sans espoir;
> Et quoi qu'on en ait dit, ma raison s'épouvante
> De ne pas le comprendre, et pourtant de le voir.
>
> . . . . .
>
> O toi que nul n'a pu connaître,
> Et n'a renié sans mentir,
> Reponds-moi, toi qui m'as fait naître
> Et demain me feras mourir!
> Puisque tu te laisses comprendre,
> Pourquoi fais-tu douter de toi?
> Quel triste plaisir peux-tu prendre
> À tenter notre bonne foi?"

But this tavern god of wine-bibbers, whom one slaps on the shoulder and treats as a comrade and jolly fellow, irritates me as the usurpation of a noble title. No, they cannot know thee, holy Being whom we behold not save in the serenity of a pure heart. Only to us that know how we may seek thee dost thou belong. The blasphemies of the man of genius must please thee more than the vulgar homage of complacent gaiety. The atheist is far rather he that misjudges thee to such a point, than he that denies thee. The despair of a Lucretius or a Byron was more after thine own heart, than this brazen-faced confidence of superficial optimism which insults while it adores thee.

I should not insist on the puerility of this plebeïan theology, did it not cause us to touch one of those phenomena of the religious consciousness which are most worthy of study—that is to say, the singular alliance sometimes established between dogmatism and frivolity. Nothing puts people so much at ease as fixed opinions in the matter of politics, religion, and literature. That which gives us rhetoric in poetry gives us in religion a need for rigorously determinate forms. People do not dream that perspicacity is the opposite of poetry and religion, which pursue an obscure and mysterious ideal. France, the only country where one amuses one's self, is essentially the country of settled opinions and limited horizons. The tendency among worldly people to take for pride the calm of the philosopher, passing from that which they regard as necessary for a tranquil life; and the facility with which persons who have lived a frivolous life become attached, on their conversion, to narrow ideas, are due to the cause indicated here. La Fontaine was converted, Boccaccio and Ariosto were not. That is perfectly simple: the tales of La Fontaine are licentious, those of Boccaccio and Ariosto are only charming. Great thought knows no remorse, and great art has never to repent.

The clumsiness of the French spirit when the infinite is in question, the timidity which causes that spirit—powerless to deny or to understand—to attempt to have a share of the infinite, does not however date from our own days. Voltaire was the first to exhibit the singular combination of a very irreligious and even somewhat immoral turn of imagination with a weighty and sound philosophy. Voltaire is a nimble rather than a daring spirit. M. Béranger's laughter remained equally far distant from true delicacy; his careless air always retained some of that affectation of gallantry which at times renders the Frenchman so ridiculous to the foreigner. His fashion of treating women resembles his religion; it is not only devoid of all distinction, but even of all wit and urbanity. The offensive familiarities which he permitted himself with his reader were also due to the same cause—that is to say, the want of reserve which prevented him from ever leaving the limbo of vulgarity. Seeking the favour of a certain public which loves to be taken unceremoniously, he encouraged it to be on good terms with him, and not take him too seriously. He also fell more heavily than any one else into the pitfalls that yawn beneath the feet of those who have no horror of vapid opinions. There is nothing more fatal to mental development than an overmastering sympathy. Béranger had only one object of hatred, the sanctimonious Restoration, the association—a very foolish one in fact—of the throne and the altar. That hatred was his ruin. It is never good to desire something so much that everything else is a matter of indifference, and is even subservient. The wholly disenchanted life created by the eighteenth century, the deplorable tradition of which was dominant until 1815, and the extreme aridity of the society which emerged from the later Revolutionary epoch, did not revolt him. Delivered from the nobleman and the priest, it troubled him little that the two things which these classes represent—often, I confess, very badly—should suffer some loss.

Do we now understand why M. Béranger has obtained his certificate of orthodoxy, and why the country, that is most essentially Catholic, has chosen for her national poet the superficial mocker at the dogmas of Catholicism, the unmannerly detractor of its worship and observances? His apparent frivolity has been his excuse. A grain of buffoonery has procured his pardon for everything. Let those reputations which have become national be examined, and it will be seen that there is scarcely one into which a little of the favour attached to bad taste does not enter in this way. Good manners, on the contrary, which are necessarily aristocratic, in the sense that they imply respect for one's self and for others, are always displeasing and bring unpopularity. How has it not served Henry IV. that he was a libertine! This good land of France was unable to resist the seduction of a king who was also a boon companion, who respected no woman, and wore an air of easy familiarity.

Some years ago the public revelled in the correspondence of a celebrated man, in which he confessed to being a gambler, an adventurer, and a scamp. That did not cause any prejudice, and when it was announced that he had had a Christian end, everybody felt edified. I imagine that something of this sort will happen to M. Béranger. Legend will depict him at confession, exchanging a hearty laugh with his *curé*. He himself delighted in that frightful type of Rabelaisian *curé*, the *Vicar of Wakefield* of the Gallic race, the ideal of whom has been caressed by all our song-writers, and whom M. Béranger has exhibited, in one of his most piquant lyrics, drinking in a tavern and damning nobody.

Observe at what price all things have been permitted to him. France loves drunken impiety; she does not tolerate purified religion. M. Béranger enchanted her by scoffing at the beliefs for which she caused the Massacre of St. Bartholomew, traversed a century of civil war, and instituted tortures and proscriptions. Protestantism amassed a wealth of wrath against her; France in a frenzy applauded or tolerated atrocious persecutors, Foucault, Bâville, Saint-Florentin, worthy of the same execration as the Carriers and the Fouquier-Tinvilles, at the very hour when she was adoring Voltaire and reading *La Pucelle* on the quiet. Ah! if the pastors of the wilderness had only resolved to imitate the *curé* of whom M. Béranger was to sing, they would not have been rebels. But they were grave, independent, and austere; and they were therefore hanged or broken on the wheel, while those who hanged them were received on their return to Paris as very honourable men. In this country a man is compromised if he gives expression to any ideas of his own about religion; he is lost if he mentions the name of Spinoza without accompanying it with an anathema. But the libertine is sacred; the Code protects him, and he has a right to consideration. Let the thinker claim the inviolate rights of science and free inquiry, and he is an innovator, and, if he has readers, a dangerous man. But were he pleased, instead of that, to sing the charms of Lisette and laugh at sacred things with glass in hand, the clergy would turn out to be odious retrograde enemies of light, should they venture to oppose him; and the shade of the national poet would arise to warn all the joyous topers of France that liberty was menaced, and the principles of '89 in danger.

There results from all this a lesson for the young poets who, according to a prediction already a year or two old, cannot fail to give lustre to the second half of our century. It is a mistake to be too delicate. Instead of studying with fear and trembling the problem that others find so clear, be vulgar, laugh, make drinking-songs, flatter popular delusions, and all will be forgiven you. Slightly expurgated editions of your works will put you within the reach of all. Portraits of you will be published on which young maidens will smile. You will be at once the tavern poet and the family poet, the poet of middle-class dinner-parties and the poet for evening reading. You will enjoy, to quote the words of the editor of the *Béranger des Familles*, "That fabulous immortality which the gratitude of a people accords to those that have sincerely loved it." You will be national. That is perfectly simple; each country seeks the liberty which best suits it. Liberty of thought and belief has no value, save for those that are capable of believing and thinking. Liberty of Philistine Epicureanism, on the other hand, is of the first importance in a land where the pursuit of a certain vulgar happiness has become the cause of political revolutions, the inspiration of the Muse, the care, and, in a sense, the religion of all.

INTOLERANCE IN SCEPTICISM

(M. FEUERBACH AND THE NEW HEGELIAN SCHOOL).

EVERY important evolution in the field of human opinions is worthy of interest, even though we may not value very highly the essential ideas which bring it to pass. It is on this account that no one who is devoted to critical research, can refuse to pay attention to the works of the Neo-Hegelian school on Christianity, although these works may not always possess a genuinely scientific character, and may often have more of the fancy of the humorist in them than the severe method of the historian.

The antipathy of the new German school to Christianity dates from Goethe. Pagan by nature, and above all by his literary system, Goethe could have but little taste for the æsthetics which has substituted the *gausapa* of the slave for the toga of the freeman, the sickly virgin for the Venus of antiquity, and for the ideal perfection of the human body represented by the gods of Greece, the emaciated image of an executed man hanging by four nails. Inaccessible to fear and unmoved by weeping, Jupiter was indeed the god of that great man; and we feel no surprise when we see him place the colossal head of his god before his bed in the light of the rising sun, so that he may bow himself in prayer before it.

Hegel has not pronounced less decidedly in favour of the religious ideal of the Greeks, and against the intrusion of

Syrian or Galilean elements. To him the legend of Christ seems conceived on the same system as the Alexandrine biography of Pythagoras. It passes, according to him, into the domain of the most vulgar reality, and in no measure into a poetic world; it is a mixture of paltry mysticism and colourless chimeras, such as we find among fantastic people unpossessed of fine imagination. In his eyes the Old and the New Testaments have no æsthetic value.

It was this same thesis which so many times aroused the ire of Heinrich Heine. The learned school of pure *Teutonists* (Gervinius, Lassen, etc.), who, to quote Ozanam's expression, cannot forgive Christian meekness for having spoiled their bellicose ancestors, have had a great deal to say of the same kind. But M. Louis Feuerbach[1] certainly represents the most advanced, if not the most serious expression of the antipathy of which we speak; and should the nineteenth century see the end of the world, it would be he, without a doubt, whom we should have to call the Antichrist.

M. Feuerbach all but defines Christianity as a perversion of human nature, and Christian æsthetics as a perversion of the innermost instincts of the heart. The perpetual lamentations of Christians over their sins appear to

[1] The most characteristic of M. Feuerbach's writings, and of those of the Neo-Hegelian school, have been collected and translated by M. Hermann Ewerbeck in two volumes, one entitled, *Qu'est-ce que la Religion?* the other, *Qu'est-ce que la Bible d'après la nouvelle philosophie allemande?* (Paris 1850). It is unfortunate that the translator, whose disinterestedness is worthy of praise, should have included with writings which perhaps it is good to know, some valueless fragments, of which some can in no sense be taken seriously. (English readers can also refer to the translation entitled the *Essence of Christianity*, by Marian Evans (George Eliot), published in London, 1853.—*Translator's Note.*)

him the most intolerable childishness, the humility and poverty of monastic life are for him only the worship of dirt and ugliness; and he would willingly say with Rutilius Numatianus:[1] "Is this sect then, I ask you, less fatal than the poison of Circe? Circe changed bodies, but here we have spirits changed into swine."

Let us say distinctly, and with the more assurance in that we only wish to oppose æsthetic considerations with views of the same kind, that the critical spirit cannot admit so absolute a judgment. Wherever there is originality, a true expansion of some of the instincts of human nature, we must meet with beauty and adore it. You may, if you will, call this æsthetics sad, but it has its boldness and grandeur. Heavy and rustic, if you compare it with the learned fables of Greece, this legend, independently of its incomparable morality, possesses, even when we look at it only from the point of view of art, a great charm of simplicity. Once on a time good taste refused the name of beauty to anything which did not attain perfection of form. Such is no longer our *criterium;* we pardon barbarism, wherever we discover in it the expression of a new manner of feeling, and the very breath of the human soul.

Would to God that M. Feuerbach had plunged in richer sources of life than those of his exclusive and overbearing Teutonism! Ah! if, seated on the ruins of Mount Palatine or Mount Cœlius, he had heard the sound of the eternal bells linger and die away upon the desert hills where once stood Rome; or if, on the lonely beach of Lido, he had heard the chimes of St. Mark's expiring on the lagoons; if he had beheld Assisi and its mystic marvels, its double basilica, and the great legend of the second Christ of the Middle Ages drawn by the pencil of Cimabue and Giotto;

[1] See Note XXIII.

if he had looked with long and tender gaze on the virgins of Perugino, or had seen at San Domenico of Siena, St. Catherine in her ecstasy,—no, M. Feuerbach would not thus cast opprobrium on one half of human poetry, or exclaim against it, as though he wished to throw far from him the phantom of Iscariot.

M. Feuerbach's errors are nearly always in his æsthetic judgments. He often presents his facts with sufficient delicacy, but they are ever criticised with revolting severity, and with the prejudiced opinion that everything Christian is either ugly, atrocious, or ridiculous. One can be in agreement with him upon many points of detail, without sharing any of his views on the general morality of history. Yes, the great difference between Hellenism and Christianity is that Hellenism is natural and Christianity supernatural. The religions of antiquity were only the State, the family, art, and morality, raised to a high and poetic expression; they knew of neither renunciation nor sacrifice, they did not divide up life; for them the distinction between the sacred and the profane did not exist. Antiquity in its manner of feeling is direct and simple; Christianity, on the contrary, ever on its guard against nature, seeks after the strange and the paradoxical. For it, abstinence is worth more than enjoyment; happiness must be sought in its opposite; the wisdom of the flesh, that is to say natural wisdom, is foolishness, the foolishness of the Cross is wisdom. Are the writings of St. Paul, from one end to the other, anything else than a calculated overturning of human sense, a commentary in anticipation of the *Credo quia absurdum* of Tertullian? The distinction between the flesh and the spirit, which was unknown to the ancients, for whom human life kept its harmonious unity, lit from that time the war between man and his self, which eighteen centuries have failed to quell.

Hence strange disorders, counterbalanced by admirable moral conquests. Aberrations, such as antiquity had only known in the forms of its worship that were most infected with superstition, became contagious. Upon what was the meditation of Christian piety, the imagination of ecstatic enthusiasts, exercised by preference? Was it upon the Trinity, upon the Holy Spirit, or upon these dialectic dogmas which we regard as sealed formulæ? No; it was upon the little child, the *Santo Bambino* in its cradle. There was no saint who had not kissed its feet; St. Catherine of Siena was espoused to it, and one such as she took it in her arms. It was upon the Passion, upon the suffering Christ that they mused. Not a saint but what had felt the imprint of his pierced hands, of his open side. St. Magdalen of Pazzi saw him in a dream, shedding through his five wounds five fountains of blood; another beheld his heart bleeding and transfixed. It was upon Mary; Mary sufficed to satisfy the need of loving for ten centuries of ascetics. Mary has entered of full right into the Trinity; she far excels that third forgotten person without lovers or adorers, the Holy Spirit. She completes the divine family, for it would have been a marvellous thing had the womanly element in Christianity failed to succeed in mounting to the very bosom of God, and had it not enthroned the Mother between the Father and the Son.[1]

At the same time the ethical ideal changed, but in a sense was heightened and ennobled. Paganism, taking human nature as upright and good, consecrated it as a

[1] The representations of the *Incoronata*, where Mary, placed between the Father and the Son, receives the crown from the hands of the former, and the homage of the latter, exhibit the true Trinity of Christian piety.

whole, even in its evil parts; there was the mistake and the error. Christianity, on its side, by casting too absolute an anathema upon nature, prepared that taste for the abject and the mean which seduced the Middle Ages. The man of antiquity, Aristides or Solon, peacefully swims in the current of life; his perfection and his imperfections are those of our nature. The Christian man mounts upon the column of Stylites, abstracts himself from everything, and, only using the surface of our world because it is necessary to have something to stand upon, suspends himself between Heaven and Earth. The ideal of beauty degenerates in purity, but gains in depth. The ideal is no longer ennobled nature, the perfection of the real, the flower of that which is; the ideal is the anti-natural, it is the body of a dead God, it is the *Addolorata* pallid and veiled, it is the Magdalen torturing her flesh. Had any one proposed to the ancient artist one of the subjects dear to Christianity, the Virgin or the Crucifix, he would have spurned it as impossible. *Ceres Dolorosa* is beautiful as a woman and as a mother, but the Virgin!—her conception and her travail are supernatural, her brothers are the angels; here below she has neither sister nor husband. So too when Christian art, returning to profane tradition, goes to seek for types of the Madonna at Albano or Transtevere, it will be a sacrilege against which the Christian conscience will righteously protest. Prometheus nailed upon his rock is beautiful still; but Jesus on his cross! . . . If you seek to realise in that emaciated body the ideal of the human form, the harmonious proportions of Dionysius or Apollo, if you give to that thorn-crowned head the lofty calmness of the Olympian Jupiter, it is a misconception,—almost an impiety. The Byzantine Church was consistent when it tenaciously maintained the thesis of the material plainness of Christ. He must be represented as thin, emaciated, bleeding, so that his bones may be counted, that he may be taken for a leper, an earthworm and not a man. *Putavimus eum quasi leprosum. . . . Non est species ei neque decor. . . . Despectum novissimum virorum, virum dolorum et scientem infirmitatem.*

Yes, all this is strange, new, unheard of; and St. Paul was right in calling it scandal and infatuation. But all this is of human nature itself; it has all come at its own time, at its own day it has gone forth from the eternal germ of things beautiful. A great modification has been at work in human nature; a warm and humid wind has blown from the south, and slackened its rigidity. Love has changed its object; to enthusiasm for beauty has succeeded enthusiasm for suffering, and the apotheosis of the Man of Sorrows acquainted with grief, of the Divine Leper, to use Bossuet's words.[1]

It is by a grave misunderstanding that antiquity is reproached with materialism. Antiquity was neither materialistic nor spiritualistic, it was human. Ancient life, serene and gracious as it was within its narrow limits, was wanting in open outlook on the infinite. Consider those charming little houses at Pompeii; like them it is gay and complete, but yet narrow and without horizon. Everywhere are repose and joy, everywhere images of happiness and pleasure. But with those things we are no longer satisfied. We no longer conceive life without sadness. Full as we are of our supernatural ideas and our thirst for the infinite, that limited art, that simple morality, that system of life so carefully finished in all its parts, seem

1 Never has this side of Christianity been treated with more vigour and originality than in Bossuet's admirable sermons on the Passion and on the Compassion of the Holy Virgin.

to us of a narrow realism. Castor and Pollux, Diana and Minerva are for us cold images, since they represent healthy and normal nature. But let us be on our guard; grand airs of abstinence and sacrifice are often nothing more than a refinement of instincts which are contented with their opposites. In reality Christian spiritualism is much more sensual than what is known as ancient materialism,[1] and sometimes bears a resemblance to relaxation. The Dorian Artemis, that masculine maiden who touched the heart of the severe Hippolytus, has always seemed to me more austere than the *dear St. Elizabeth* who made M. de Montalambert[2] so desperately amorous. Those who have visited Naples have had an opportunity of seeing, at the Chapel of the Pietà de' Sangri, a *Pudicizia* robed in a long veil which covers the whole person in such a way that it allows one to divine, under the marble folds, a form made more attractive by mystery. On the other hand, there is in the Vatican Museum an antique Modesty, half nude, but veiled with severe beauty. Which do you believe is in reality the more chaste? Greece with an exquisite tact perceived in all things perfect proportion, the fugitive *nuance* that one seizes for a moment but cannot retain. Proportion, in point of fact, appears cold and wearisome in the long run; we grow tired of symmetry and good taste. Perfectly pure types no longer suffice; we yearn for the strange, the superhuman, the supernatural.

It is not the fault of individuals or systems that religious feelings should undergo these profound revolutions. It is

[1] It should be understood that I only speak of the pure and lofty antiquity of Greece. I ought also to observe that we are discussing what is, before all else, a question of æsthetics and taste, a question which must be settled by the examination of works of poetry and fine art.

[2] See Note XXIV.

not willingly that man quits the smooth and easy paths of the plain for the wild and rugged mountain peaks. It is because measure and proportion, by only representing the finite, grow insufficient for the heart that aspires to the infinite. Whilst humanity is prisoned within precise and narrow limits, it is at rest and happy in its mediocrity; but when, grown exacting and unhappy, and yet in a sense nobler, it gives ear to vaster needs, it prefers, both in art and morality, suffering, and unsated desire, and the vague and painful feeling that is born of the infinite, to the full and complete satisfaction afforded by a finished work.

But if there be an incurable evil, thanks to God it is this! The sensitive are unhappy, but we cannot cure sensitivity. We can recognise a broken spirit, but we cannot restore its strength. And then deviation has so many charms, and rectitude is so fastidious! An ancient temple incontestably possesses a purer beauty than a Gothic church, and yet we pass hours in the latter without feeling weary, while we cannot remain for five minutes in the former without being bored. That, according to M. Feuerbach, proves that our taste is perverted. But how can it be helped?

If M. Feuerbach had confined himself to pointing out these contrasts calmly and tenderly; if, content to observe with interest the alternatives of human feeling, he had not opposed to the often gratuitous enthusiasm of the believer a still more gratuitous hatred, we should have no right to deal very severely with him. But the impartial philosopher cannot assent to the absolute condemnation which M. Feuerbach hurls upon eighteen centuries of the history of the human mind; for, if he reflects, he sees that it is the human mind itself which is standing its trial. It serves no good purpose to pour out his hatred upon the words, "Christianity," "theology," etc. For who, after all, made

Christianity? Who created theology? Humanity accepts no chains other than those which it has put upon itself. Humanity has done all, and—we wish to believe it—has done all well.

Besides, it is not only supernaturalism that falls under the criticism of the new German school. M. Feuerbach and all the philosophers of this school unhesitatingly declare that theism, natural religion—in a word, every system that admits anything of a transcendental nature, must be put upon the same footing as supernaturalism. To believe in God and the immortality of the soul is, in his eyes, quite as superstitious as to believe in the Trinity and in miracles. To him criticism of Heaven is only criticism of the earth; theology must become anthropology. Every consideration of the higher world, every glance cast by man beyond himself and reality, all religious feeling, under whatever form it may manifest itself, is but a delusion. Not to be severe towards such a philosophy, we wish to see in it nothing more than a misapprehension. M. Feuerbach has written at the beginning of the second edition of his *Essence of Christianity:* "By this book I have embroiled myself with God and the world." We believe it to be slightly his own fault that it is so, and that, had he wished it, God and the world would have pardoned him. Led away by that bad tone which reigns in the German universities, and which I should willingly term the *pedantry of boldness*, many upright minds and honest souls have attributed to themselves the honours of atheism. When a German boasts of being impious, he must never be taken at his word. The German is not capable of being irreligious; religion, that is to say, aspiration towards the ideal world, is the very foundation of his nature. When he wishes to be atheistical, he is devoutly so, with a sort of unction. How, if you practise the worship of the beautiful and the true, if the sanctity of morality speaks to your heart, if all beauty and all truth bear you to the home of holy life; how, if, when you have come there you veil your head, and purposely overawe thought and language, so that no limited utterance may escape you in front of the infinite,—how, I say, do you dare to speak of atheism? If indeed your faculties in simultaneous vibrations have never given forth that one great strain that we call God, I have nothing more to say; you are wanting in the essential and characteristic element of our nature.

To those who, placing themselves at the point of view of substance, ask me, "Does this God exist, or does he not?" "Oh God!" I make reply, "it is he that is, and all the rest that but appears to be." Even supposing that for us philosophers another word were preferable, and without taking into account the fact that abstract words do not express real existence with sufficient clarity, there would be an immense inconvenience in thus cutting ourselves away from all the poetic sources of the past, and in separating ourselves by our language from the simple folk who worship so well in their own way.

The word God being respected by humanity, having for it a long-acquired right, and having been employed in all beautiful poetry, to abandon it would be to overthrow all habits of language. Tell the simple to pass their lives in aspiration after truth, and beauty, and moral goodness; and your words will be meaningless to them. Tell them to love God, and not to offend God; and they will understand you perfectly. God, Providence, Immortality, are good old words; they are a little clumsy perhaps, but philosophy will interpret them in senses that will ever grow more and more refined, though it will never replace them with advantage. Under one form or another God will always be the sum of our supra-sensible needs, the *category of the ideal* (that is to say, the form under which we conceive the ideal), as space and time are the *categories of matter* (that is to say, the forms under which we conceive matter). In other words, man placed before things beautiful, good, or true, comes forth from himself and, suspended by a celestial charm, humiliates his puny personality, and is exalted in rapture. And what is this, if not worship?

MARCUS AURELIUS.[1]

It was with great pleasure that I accepted the invitation to come and exchange some ideas with you in this famous Institution, devoted as it is to scientific and philosophical studies of the highest order. Of this island, in which I have so many friends, and which I have visited so tardily, I dreamed in my childhood. I am a French Briton. In our old books I used to see England always called the Isle of Saints; and, in fact, all our saints of Armorican Brittany, those saints of dubious orthodoxy who, were they recalled to life, would be on better terms with us than with the Jesuits, came from the island of Britain. In their chapel I have been shown the stone trough in which they crossed the sea. Of all races, the Breton race is the one which has ever taken religion most seriously. Even when the progress of reflection has shown us some articles to be modified in the list of things that once on a time we held for certain, we never break with the symbol under which we first tasted the ideal. For faith, as we understand it, does not reside in obscure metaphysical propositions; it dwells in the affirmations of the heart. The theme which I have chosen to treat with you is not then one of those subtilities which divide men from each other, but one of those subjects, dear to the soul, which bring together and unite. I

[1] A lecture delivered at the Royal Institution, London, April 16th, 1880.

shall speak to you of that book all-resplendent with the divine spirit, of that manual of the resigned life which has been left to us by the most pious of men, Marcus Aurelius Antoninus Cæsar. It is the glory of monarchs that the most irreproachable model of virtue is to be found in their ranks, and that the finest lessons of patience and detachment from the world have come from a condition of life which one easily supposes to be given up to all the seductions of pleasure and vanity.

I.

Hereditary wisdom on the throne has ever been a rare thing. In history I only see two striking examples—in India, the succession of three Mongol emperors, Baber, Humayun, and Akbar; in Rome, at the head of the vastest empire which has ever been, the two illustrious reigns of Antoninus Pius and Marcus Aurelius. Of these two last, Antoninus was, in my opinion, the greater. His goodness did not involve him in the commission of faults; he was not tormented by the inward malady which pitilessly gnawed the heart of his adopted son. This strange malady, this unquiet study of one's self, this demon of scrupulosity, this fever of perfection, are all signs of a nature less strong than distinguished. As the finest thoughts are those that remain unwritten, Antoninus had, in this respect also, a superiority over Marcus Aurelius; but let us add that we should be ignorant of Antoninus, had Marcus Aurelius not handed down for us that exquisite portrait of his adoptive father, in which he seems to have set himself by humility to depict the image of a man still better than himself.

He too it is who has traced out for us, in the First Book of his *Meditations*, that admirable background through which move in a celestial light the noble and pure forms of his father, his mother, his grandfather, and his masters. Thanks to Marcus Aurelius, we can understand how those old Roman families, which had seen the reign of the bad emperors, still kept their uprightness, their dignity, their justice, their civic spirit, and—if I may say so—their republicanism. They lived in admiration of Cato, Brutus, Thrasea, and the great Stoics whose souls had never bowed down under tyranny. The rule of Domitian was abhorrent to them; the sages who had traversed it without flinching were honoured as heroes. The advent of the Antonines was only the success to power of the society of sages, whose just wrath has been transmitted to us by Tacitus, a society of sages formed by the union of all those whom the despotism of the first Cæsars had revolted.

The salutary principle of adoption had made the imperial court of the second century a true nursery of virtue. The noble and skilful Nerva, by laying down this principle, assured the happiness of the human race for nearly a hundred years, and gave to the world the finest century of progress known to history. Sovereignty, thus held in common by a group of elect men who deputed or shared it, according to the needs of the moment, lost a part of that attraction which renders it so dangerous. The sovereign ascended the throne without having intrigued for it, but also without owing any duties to his birth or to a kind of divine right. He came to it disabused, weary of men, and after long preparation. The empire was a civic burden, which men took upon themselves when their time arrived; and no one dreamed of anticipating that time. Marcus Aurelius was marked out for it at so youthful an age, that the idea of reigning scarcely had for him any beginning, and did not exercise a moment's seduction upon him. At the age of eight, when he was already *Praesul* of the Salian priests, Hadrian remarked the gentle sad child, and loved him for his natural goodness, his docility, his incapacity for falsehood. At eighteen he was assured of the empire. For twenty-two years he awaited it patiently. On the evening when Antoninus, feeling death near, gave *Æquanimitas* as the pass-word to the tribune on duty, and caused to be borne into the chamber of his adopted son the golden statue of Fortune which had ever to stand in the Emperor's apartment, Marcus Aurelius felt neither surprise nor delight. Long since he had wearied of joys without having tasted them; by the depth of his philosophy he had seen their absolute vanity.

The great drawback of practical life, and that which renders it unsupportable to the man of superior character, lies in this,—that if ideal principles are carried into it, good qualities become faults—so much so indeed that very often the perfect man has less success in it than he whose motives are egoism or common routine. Three or four times the virtue of Marcus Aurelius almost brought about his ruin. It caused him to commit a first fault by persuading him to associate with himself in the empire Lucius Verus, a frivolous and worthless man. Prodigies of kindness and delicacy were required to prevent him from indulging in disastrous follies. The wise emperor, grave and studious, carried about with him in his litter the foolish colleague whom he had taken to himself. He always persisted in taking him seriously; he was not once revolted by the tiresome companionship. Like many people who have been very well trained, Marcus Aurelius was under an unceasing self-discipline; his habits were the result of a general scheme of deportment and dignity. Souls of this order, whether to avoid causing pain to others, whether out of respect for human nature, do not resign themselves to an avowal that they behold evil. Their life is a perpetual dissimulation.

According to some, he must have dissembled to himself, since, in his familiar colloquy with the gods on the banks of the Gran, he—speaking of a spouse unworthy of him—thanked them for having granted him "a woman so complacent, so affectionate, so simple." Elsewhere I have shown that on this point the patience, or, if you will, the weakness of Marcus Aurelius has been somewhat exaggerated. Faustina had her wrongs; the greatest of them was the aversion which she bore to her husband's friends. As it was these friends who wrote history, she underwent her punishment before posterity. But a careful criticism has not much trouble here in demonstrating the exaggerations of the legend. Everything leads to the conviction that Faustina at first found happiness and affection in that villa at Lorium, or in the beautiful retreat at Lanuvium on the lower slopes of the Alban Mount, which Marcus Aurelius described to his master Fronto as an abode full of the purest joys. And then she grew weary of so much wisdom. Let us say all; the beautiful aphorisms of Marcus Aurelius, his austere virtue, his perpetual melancholy might well seem tedious to a young capricious woman, of ardent temperament and wondrous loveliness. He understood it, suffered from it, and held his peace. Faustina always remained "his very good and very faithful spouse." Even after her death he could not be induced to abandon this pious fiction. In a bas-relief, still to be seen at Rome in the Museum of the Capitol, Faustina is represented as being borne up to Heaven by Fame, while the excellent emperor follows her from earth with a gaze full of tenderness. In his latter days it would seem as though he had come to delude himself, and to forget all. But what a struggle he must have gone through to come to that! During long years a heart sickness slowly consumed him. That despairing effort which is the very essence of his philosophy, that passion for renunciation, at times pushed almost to sophistry, hid beneath them an immense wound. How necessary it must have been to say farewell to happiness, in order to arrive at such excesses! Never will men understand all the suffering of that poor blighted heart or the bitterness which lay masked behind that pale countenance, always calm and nearly always smiling. True it is that the farewell to happiness is the beginning of wisdom, and the surest way of finding happiness. There is nothing so sweet as the return of joy which follows the renunciation of joy, nothing so keen, so deep, so full of charm as the enchantment of the disenchanted.

Historians, more or less imbued with that political tendency which believes itself superior, because it is not suspected of philosophy, have naturally sought to prove that so perfect a man was a bad administrator, and a sovereign of only moderate ability. It does, in truth, appear that Marcus Aurelius sinned more than once through excess of indulgence. But never was a reign more fruitful of reforms and progress. Public assistance, founded by Nerva and Trajan, received at his hands admirable developments. New colleges for the children so assisted were established; the alimentary procurators became functionaries of the first importance, and were selected with great care. For the needs of young girls of poor birth the Institution of Young Faustinians was founded. The principle that the State has duties, in some measure paternal, towards its members (a principle which it will be our duty to remember with gratitude even when it has been superseded), this principle,

I say, was proclaimed in the world for the first time by Trajan and his successors. Neither the puerile ostentation of Oriental monarchies founded on the degradation and stupidity of men, nor the pedantic pride of mediæval kingdoms founded on an exaggerated sense of heredity and a naïve faith in the rights of blood, can give us an idea of the wholly republican sovereignty of Nerva, Trajan, Hadrian, Antoninus, and Marcus Aurelius. Here we have no trace of hereditary kingship or divine right, nor anything analogous to military chieftainship. It was a kind of great civil magistracy, which had nothing resembling a court, and took from the emperor all characteristics of a private person. Marcus Aurelius, in particular, was neither little nor much of a king in the proper sense of the word. His fortune was immense, but it was wholly spent in the public good. His aversion to the Cæsars, whom he regarded as a species of Sardanapali, magnificent, debauched, and cruel, is at every instant apparent. The civility of his manners was extreme; to the Senate he rendered all its ancient importance. When he was at Rome he never missed a sitting, and only quitted his place when the Consul had pronounced the formula, *Nihil vos moramur patres conscripti.* In nearly every year of his reign he waged war, and waged it well; although in it he only found weariness. His dull campaigns against the Quadi and the Marcommani were conducted very efficiently; his distaste for them did not prevent him from using the most conscientious endeavours.

It was in the course of one of these expeditions that, when encamped on the banks of the Gran in the midst of the monotonous plains of Hungary, he wrote the finest pages of the exquisite book which has revealed his whole soul to us. It is probable that he early acquired the habit of keeping a private journal of his reflections. In it he inscribed the maxims to which he had recourse for support, reminiscences of his favourite authors, passages from the moralists who most appealed to him, principles which during the day had sustained him, and sometimes the reproaches which his scrupulous conscience thought it necessary to address to itself.

"Men seek solitary retreats, rural farm-houses, sea-shores, mountains; like others, thou lovest to dream of these pleasant things. To what good end, seeing that it is permitted thee every hour to withdraw into thine own soul? Nowhere hath man a more tranquil retreat; above all, if he have in himself these things the contemplation of which suffices to give him peace. Know then to enjoy every day this retreat, and there renew thy strength. Let there be there short fundamental maxims which on the instant will give serenity to thy soul, and put thee in a fit state to support with resignation the world to which thou must return."

During the dreary Northern winters this consolation became still more necessary for him. He was nearly sixty years of age. With him old age was premature. One evening all the images of his pious youth came back to his memory once more; and he passed some delicious hours in computing what he owed to each of the virtuous beings who had surrounded him.

"The examples of my grandfather Verus: gentleness of manners and invincible patience. Qualities which were esteemed in my father, the memory he has left me: modesty and manly character.

"To imitate my mother in her piety, her well-doing; like her, to abstain not only from doing evil but even from conceiving the thought of it, and to lead her frugal life, which so little resembled the habitual luxury of the rich."

Then in succession appear to him Diognetus, who inspired him with a taste for philosophy, and made pleasant in his eyes the pallet, the simple covering of skin, and the whole outfit of Hellenic discipline; Junius Rusticus, who taught him to avoid all affectation of elegance in style, and lent him the Discourses of Epictetus; Apollonius of Chalchis, who realised the Stoic ideal of extreme firmness and perfect sweetness; the grave and good Sextus of Chæronea; Alexander the grammarian, who administered reproof with so refined a courtesy; Fronto, who taught him "the envy, duplicity, and hypocrisy that are in a tyrant, and what cruelty can exist in a patrician's heart;" his brother Severus, who made him acquainted with Thrasea, Helvidius, Cato, Dion, and Brutus, and gave him the idea of a free state "where natural equality of the citizens and equality of their rights exist, of a kingdom which places before all else respect for the freedom of its citizens;" and, dominating all the others by his immaculate grandeur, Antoninus, his adoptive father, whose image he depicts for us with passionate gratitude and affection.

"I thank the gods," he says in conclusion, "for having given me good grandfathers, good parents, a good sister, good masters, and in those around me, my relatives and my friends, people almost all filled with goodness. Never have I allowed myself to be wanting in respect for them; by my natural disposition I might occasionally have committed some irreverence, but the bounty of the gods has not permitted such a circumstance to have presented itself. Nay more, I am indebted to the gods for having kept pure the flower of my youth, for my having been brought up under the law of a prince and a father who cleansed my soul from all vain glory, who made me understand how it is possible, even while living in a palace, to pass from guards, from splendid raiment, from torches and statues, who taught me finally that a prince may almost shrink his life within the limits of that of a private citizen, without on that account showing less majesty and vigour, when it is a question of being emperor and treating affairs of state. It was by their favour that I met a brother whose behaviour was a constant exhortation to keep watch upon myself, while at the same time his deference and attachment were to be the joy of my heart. Thanks to the gods again, I hastened to raise those who had superintended my education to the honours which they seemed to desire. It was they who introduced me to Apollonius, Rusticus, and Maximus, and offered me in so clear a light the image of a life conforming to nature. True, I have not reached the goal; but it is my own fault. If my bodily health has held out so well under the severe life which I lead; if, despite my frequent disagreements with Rusticus, I have never gone beyond bounds or done anything of which I have had to repent; if my mother, whose fate it was to die young, was nevertheless able to pass her last years near me; if, every time that I have desired to succour some poor or afflicted person, I have never heard it said that money failed me; if I have never myself been in need of receiving anything from any one; if I have a wife of such a character, complacent, affectionate, simple; if I have found so many capable persons for the education of my children; if, at the beginning of my passion for philosophy, I did not become the prey of some sophist;—it is to the gods that I owe all these things. Yes, so many blessings can only be the effect of the assistance of the gods, and of a happy fortune."

This divine candour inspires every page. Never did a

man write more simply for himself, for the sole purpose of relieving his heart with no witness save God alone. There is not a shadow of system; Marcus Aurelius has, properly speaking, no philosophy. Although he may owe nearly everything to Stoicism transformed by the Roman spirit, he is of no school. For our taste he shows too little curiosity, in so far as he does not know all that a contemporary of Ptolemy and Galen ought to know. Some of his opinions concerning the system of the world are not on the level of the most advanced science of his time. But his moral thought, being thus free from all bonds with a system, achieves a singular loftiness. Even the author of the *Imitation*, though little engaged in the quarrels of schools, scarcely attains such a height; for his manner of feeling is essentially Christian. Take away the Christian dogmas, and his book no longer retains more than a part of its charm. The book of Marcus Aurelius, having no dogmatic base, will keep its freshness for ever. All, from the atheist, or the man who believes himself one, to him who is most absorbed in the special beliefs of some form of religion, can find therein fruits of edification. It is the most purely human book that has ever existed. It deals with no controversial topic. In theology Marcus Aurelius floats between pure deism, polytheism interpreted in a physical sense after the manner of the Stoics, and a species of cosmic pantheism. He does not incline much more to one of these hypotheses than to another, and he makes use indifferently of the three vocabularies, deist, polytheist, and pantheist. His considerations have ever two faces, according as God and the soul have or have not reality. It is the reasoning that we use at every hour, for if it be the completest materialism that is in the right, we who have believed in the true and the good shall not be more duped than the others. If idealism be in the right, we shall have been the true sages, and have been so in the only fitting fashion, that is to say, without any selfish expectation, without having counted on a reward.

II.

Here we touch one of the great secrets of moral philosophy and religion. Marcus Aurelius has no speculative philosophy, his theology is altogether contradictory, he has no definitely fixed opinion concerning the soul and immortality. How was it that he was profoundly moral, without the beliefs that are now regarded as the foundations of morality? How was he eminently religious, without having professed any of the dogmas of that which we call natural religion? It is into this that I propose to inquire.

The doubts which, from the point of view of speculative reason, hover over the truths of natural religion are not, as Kant has admirably demonstrated, accidental doubts capable of being removed, belonging, as one sometimes imagines, to certain states of the human mind. Such doubts are inherent in the very nature of these truths; and it might be said without paradox that, if the doubts were dissipated, the truths which they attack would disappear at the same blow. Let us, in fact, suppose a proof direct, positive, evident to all, of future punishments and rewards; wherein would be the merit of doing good? It would only be madmen who from gaiety of heart would run to their own damnation. A host of base souls would work out salvation with their cards on the table; in a measure they would force the hand of the Almighty. Who is there that cannot see that in such a system there is no longer either morality or religion? In the sphere of ethics and religion it is indispensable to believe without demonstration. It is not a question of certainty; it is a question of faith. This is what deism, with its habits of intemperate affirmation, forgets. It forgets that over-precise beliefs concerning human destiny would take away all moral merit. For our own part, if a peremptory argument of this kind were announced to us, we should act as did St. Louis, when some one spoke to him of the miraculous wafer. We should refuse to go and see. What need have we of brutal proofs which would fetter our liberty? We should fear being assimilated with those speculators in virtue, or those vulgar cravens who in the things of the soul use the gross egoism of practical life. In the first days which followed the belief in the resurrection of Jesus, this feeling came to light in the most touching manner. The true loving friends, the delicate of soul loved better to believe without proof than to see. "Happy are they that have not seen, and yet have believed," became the phrase of the situation. Beautiful phrase! Eternal symbol of the tender and generous idealism, which has a horror of touching with its hands that which ought to be known of the heart alone!

Our good Marcus Aurelius on this point, as on all others, was in advance of his age. He never troubled to come to an agreement with himself concerning God and the soul. As though he had read the "Critique of Practical Reason," he clearly saw that in dealing with the infinite no formula is absolute, and that in such a matter the only chance of beholding truth for once in one's life is to contradict one's self repeatedly. He resolutely severed moral beauty from all definite theology; he did not permit duty to depend on any metaphysical opinion concerning the First Cause.

Never was close union with the hidden God pushed to such an extremity of delicacy.

"Offer to the governance of the god that is within thee a virile being ripened with years, a friend of the public good, a Roman, an emperor; a soldier at his post awaiting the sound of the trumpet; a man ready to quit life without regret."

"There are many grains of incense destined for the same altar; one falleth sooner in the fire, another later; but the difference is nothing."

"Man must live according to Nature during the few days that are granted him on earth, and, when the moment to retire is come, must gently submit like an olive, which as it falleth blesseth the tree that gave it birth and giveth thanks to the branch that hath borne it."

"Everything harmoniseth with me which is harmonious with thee, O Universe. Nothing for me is too early or too late which is in due time for thee. Everything is fruit to me which thy seasons bring, O Nature; from thee are all things, in thee are all things, to thee all things return."

"O man, thou hast been a citizen in this great state; what difference doth it make to thee whether for five years or for three? For that which is conformable to the laws is just for all. Where then is the hardship, if no tyrant nor yet an unjust judge sendeth thee away from the state, but Nature who brought thee into it? It is as though a prætor who hath employed an actor dismisseth him from the stage: 'But I have not played the five acts, but only three of them.' Depart then satisfied, for he also who releaseth thee is satisfied."

Does this mean that he did not sometimes revolt against the strange destiny which has been pleased to leave alone, face to face, man with his eternal craving for devotion, for sacrifice, for heroism, and Nature with her transcendent immorality, her supreme disdain for virtue? No; at least once the absurdity, the colossal iniquity of death strikes him. But soon his temperament, wholly mortified, takes the upper hand again, and he calms himself.

"How can it be that the gods, after having arranged all things well and benevolently for mankind, have overlooked this alone, that some men, and very good men, and men who, as we may say, have had most communion with the divinity, and through pious acts and religious observances have been most intimate with the divinity, when they have once died, should never exist again, but be completely extinguished? But if this is so, rest assured that if it ought to have been otherwise the gods would have done it. For if it were just it would also be possible; and if it were according to Nature, Nature would have had it so. But because it is not so, if in fact it is not so, be thou convinced that it ought not to have been so. For thou seest, even of thyself, that in this inquiry thou art disputing with the deity; and we should not thus dispute with the gods, unless they were most excellent and most just. But if this is so, they would not have allowed anything in the ordering of the Universe to be neglected unjustly and unreasonably."

Ah! there is too much resignation here. If it is so indeed, we have a right to murmur. To say that if this world has no compensation, the man who has sacrificed himself for righteousness or truth ought to leave it contentedly, and absolve the gods, is too naïve. No, he has a right to blaspheme them! For indeed, why should they have thus abused his credulity? Why should they have put in him deceitful instincts of which he has been the honest dupe? Why should their bounty be accorded to the frivolous or wicked man? He, then, who does not deceive himself is the prudent man? But if so, then cursed be the gods who place their preferences so ill! I wish the future to be an enigma, but if there is to be no future, this world is a frightful ambush. Be careful to note that our desire is not that of the man of gross and vulgar mind. We wish neither to see the chastisement of the guilty, nor to touch the interest of our virtue. What we wish has nothing of an egoistical nature in it,—it is simply to exist, to remain in the light, to continue the thought which we have commenced, to learn more and more, and one day to enjoy that truth which we seek so laboriously, to see the triumph of the righteousness which we have loved. Nothing can be more legitimate. Indeed, the worthy emperor felt it deeply. "What! that the light of a lamp shall burn until the moment when it is extinguished, losing naught of its brilliancy; and the truth, the justice, the temperance which are in thee be extinguished with thee!" His whole life was passed in this noble hesitance. If he sinned it was through excess of piety. Less resigned, he would have been more just; for surely to ask that there may be a close and sympathetic spectator of the strife we wage in the cause of goodness and truth, is not to ask too much.

It is also possible that, had his philosophy been less exclusively ethical, had it implied a closer study of history and the universe, it would have escaped certain excesses of rigour. Like the Christian ascetics, Marcus Aurelius at times carried renunciation to aridity and subtility. One feels that the calm which never forsakes him is obtained by immense effort. Sin certainly never had any attraction for him; he had no passion to fight against. "Whatever men may do, or whatever men may say, I must of necessity be a righteous man, as the emerald might say, Whatever may be and whatever done, I must of necessity be an emerald and keep my colour." But in order to remain for ever on the ice-bound summit of Stoicism he had to do cruel violence to nature, and cut away from her more than one noble part. The perpetual repetition of the same reasonings, the thousand images under which he seeks to represent to himself the vanity of all things, the proofs, often naïve, of universal frivolity, all bear witness to the conflicts in which he had to engage, in order to extinguish all desire in himself. At times there is a touch of bitterness and sorrow resulting from all this; the reading of Marcus Aurelius fortifies, but it does not console. It leaves in the soul a void at once delicious and cruel, which we would not exchange for full satisfaction. Humility, renunciation, severity towards one's self, have never been pushed farther. Glory, that last illusion of great souls, is reduced to nullity. One must do good without being uneasy in mind as to whether anybody will know about it. He plainly sees that history will speak of him. At times he dreams of the men of the past with whom the future will associate him. "If they have played but one part, that of actors in tragedy," he says, "no one has condemned me to imitate them." The absolute mortification to which he had attained consumed the self-love in him to the very last shred.

The consequences of this austere philosophy might well have been harshness and rigour. Here it is that the rare kindliness of the nature of Marcus Aurelius shines forth in all its splendour. His severity is only towards himself. The fruit of this great tension of soul is an infinite charity. He passes his whole life studying how he may render good for evil. After some sad experience of human perversity, he only finds it in his heart at evening to write what follows: "If thou canst correct them, do so; but in the contrary case bear in mind that charity was given to thee to use towards them. The gods themselves are charitable to these beings; they assist them, so great is their bounty, to acquire health, riches, and glory. To thee it is permitted to act as do the gods." Another day men must have been very wicked, for this is what he writes upon his tablets: "Such is the order of Nature; people of this kind must of all necessity act thus. To wish it otherwise is to wish the fig-tree not to bear figs; in a very short time both thou and he shall die, and soon after your very names will no longer survive." These reflections of universal pardon constantly recur. Sometimes he almost mingles with this beautiful spirit of kindness an imperceptible smile: "The best way of avenging thyself is not to become like the wrong-doer;" or a slight touch of pride: "It is a royal thing when thou hast done good to hear evil spoken of thee." One day he has a reproach to make to himself: "Thou hast forgotten," he says, "what a holy bond of relationship uniteth every man with the human race, a relationship not of blood and birth, but participation in the same intelligence. Thou hast forgotten that the reasonable soul of each man is a god, an emanation from the Supreme Being."

In the business of life he must have been exquisite, though somewhat naïve, as very good men generally are. The nine motives for indulgence which he enumerates to himself (Book ix. 18) show his charming good humour when confronted with family difficulties, perhaps caused by his unworthy son.

"For what will the most violent man do to thee, if thou continuest to be of a kind disposition towards him, and if, as opportunity offers, thou gently admonishest him and calmly correctest his errors at the very time when he is trying to do thee harm, saying, 'Not so, my child; we are constituted by Nature for something else; I shall certainly not be injured, but thou art injuring thyself, my child.' And show him with gentle tact and by general principles that this is so, and that even bees do not do as he doth, nor any animals which are formed by Nature to be gregarious. And thou must do this neither with any irony, nor in the way of reproach, but affectionately, and without any rancour in thy soul; and not as a pedant, nor yet that any bystander may admire. Have in view him alone."

Commodus, if it be he who is in question, was doubtless little moved by this good paternal rhetoric. One of the maxims of the excellent emperor was that the wicked are unhappy, that a man is only wicked in spite of himself and through ignorance. He pitied those who were not like himself; he did not believe that he had any right to impose himself upon them.

He plainly saw the baseness of men, but he did not admit it, even to himself. This habit of voluntary blindness is the failure of great souls. The world being by no means altogether as they would have it, they deceive themselves so that they may see it other than it is. Thence ensues a slight conventionality in their judgments. In the case of Marcus Aurelius this conventionality has a somewhat irritating effect upon us. To believe him, his masters, of whom several were of very moderate ability, must all without exception have been distinguished men. One would suppose that everybody around him was virtuous. This reaches such a point that one feels constrained to ask whether this brother whom he eulogises so highly in his thanksgiving to the gods, was not Lucius Verus, his brother by adoption. It is certain that the good emperor was liable to strong illusions, when it was a question of lending his own virtues to some one else.

This habit, according to an opinion which originated in antiquity, in particular by the pen of the Emperor Julian, caused him to make an enormous mistake in not disinheriting Commodus. This is one of the things which it is easy to say at a distance, when the obstacles are no longer present, and one reasons outside the facts. It is first of all forgotten that the emperors, who since Nerva had made adoption such a fruitful political system, had no sons. Adoption, along with disinheritance of the son or grandson, was in force in the first century of the Empire, but without good results. Marcus Aurelius was evidently by principle in favour of direct heredity, in which he saw the advantages of the prevention of competition. As soon as Commodus was born in 161, he presented him alone to the legions, although he had a twin brother. Often, while he was still quite a little boy, he used to take him in his arms and perform anew this ceremony, which was a kind of proclamation. In 166 it was Lucius Verus himself who asked that the two sons of Marcus, Commodus and Annius Verus, should be made Cæsars. In 172 Commodus shared with his father the title of *Germanicus;* in 173, after the repression of the revolt of Avidius, the Senate, in order to recognise the freedom from family feeling shown by Marcus Aurelius, demanded by acclamation the empire and tribunal power for Commodus. The evil nature of the latter had already betrayed itself by more than one indication known to his preceptors; but how could they prejudice the future of a child twelve years old by some bad notes? In 176-177 his father made him *Imperator*, Consul, Augustus. This was surely an imprudence, but former acts made it inevitable. Besides Commodus still restrained himself.

In later years the evil was altogether exposed. On every page of the later books of the *Meditations* we see traces of the inward martyrdom of the excellent father, the perfect emperor, who sees a monster growing up at his side, ready to succeed him and decided upon taking in everything, by antipathy, the opposite side to that which he has seen expoused by good men. Then no doubt the thought of disinheriting Commodus must have come more than once to Marcus Aurelius. But it was too late. After having associated him in the empire, after having so many times proclaimed him before the legions to be perfect and accomplished, to come and meet the world with a declaration of his unworthiness would have been a scandal. Marcus was entrapped by his own phrases, by the conventionally charitable style which was too habitual with him. And after all Commodus was only seventeen; who could be certain that he would not improve? Even after the death of Marcus Aurelius it was still possible to hope. Commodus at first showed some intention of following the counsels of the meritorious men with whom his father had surrounded him.

It is not, then, with not having disinherited his son that one can reproach Marcus Aurelius; it is with having had a son at all. It was not his fault that the age was incapable of bearing so much wisdom. In philosophy the great emperor had placed the ideal of virtue so high, that nobody found it incumbent to pursue it. In politics his benevolent optimism enfeebled the services, more especially the army. In religion, by being too greatly attached to a state religion, the weakness of which he plainly discerned, he prepared for the violent triumph of the unofficial cult, and left hovering over his memory a reproach, unjust it is true, but one the very shadow of which should not be found in so pure a life.

Here we touch upon one of the most delicate points in the biography of Marcus Aurelius. It is unfortunately certain that some condemnations to death were pronounced and executed on the Christians under his rule. The policy of his predecessors had been constant in this respect. Trajan, Antoninus, and Hadrian himself saw in Christianity a secret and anti-social sect dreaming of the overthrow of the Empire. Like all men attached to old Roman principles, they believed themselves compelled to repress it. For that purpose there was no need of special edicts; laws against the *cœtus illiciti* and *illicita collegia* were numerous. In the most formal manner the Christians fell under the operation of these laws. It would certainly have been worthy of the wise emperor who introduced so many humane reforms, to have suppressed these edicts, which entailed cruel and unjust consequences. But one must observe at the outset that the true spirit of liberty, as we understand it, was then understood by none, and that Christianity, when it was master, practised it no better than the Pagan emperors; in the second place, that the repeal of the law relating to illicit societies would have been the ruin of the Empire, founded essentially as it was upon the principle that the state cannot permit in its bosom any society differing from it. The principle was a bad one, according to our ideas; but it is at least perfectly certain that it was the corner-stone of the Roman constitution. Marcus Aurelius, far from exaggerating it, diminished it with all his power; and one of the glories of his reign is the extension which he gave to the right of association. However, he did not go to the very root; he did not completely sweep away the laws against the *collegia illicita*, and there resulted in the provinces some infinitely regrettable applications. The reproach that we can put upon him is the same as the one we might address to the modern sovereigns who do not suppress with a stroke of the pen all laws restricting freedom of union, of association, and of the press.

From the distance at which we are, we clearly see that Marcus Aurelius, by being more completely liberal, would have shown more wisdom. It may be that Christianity left free would have developed in a less disastrous manner the theocratic and absolute spirit within it. But one cannot reproach a statesman for not having provoked a radical revolution in anticipation of events which were to happen several centuries after him. Trajan, Hadrian, Antoninus, and Marcus Aurelius could not be aware of principles of general history and political economy that have only been perceived in our own time, and that our latest revolutions could alone reveal. In any case the meekness of the good emperor is in this respect sheltered from all reproach. We have no right to be more severe in the matter than Tertullian :—

"Consult your annals," he says to the Roman magistrates, "and you will see that the princes who have used us cruelly are of those whom it is an honour to have as persecutors. On the other hand, of all the princes who have respected the laws of God and man, name one who has persecuted the Christians. We can even cite one who declared himself our protector, the wise Marcus Aurelius. If he did not openly revoke the edicts against our brothers, he destroyed their effect by the severe penalties which he established for the accusers."

We must remember that the Roman Empire was ten or twelve times greater than France, and that the emperor's responsibility for judgments passed in the provinces was very slight. We must, above all, bear in mind that Christianity did not simply claim the liberty of the different religions; all forms of faith which tolerated others were very much at ease in the Empire. What gave Christianity and Judaism a place apart was their intolerance and their exclusive spirit.

Truly, then, we have reason to wear mourning in our hearts for Marcus Aurelius. With him philosophy was on the throne. For a moment, thanks to him, the world has been governed by the best and greatest man of his age. Terrible decadence followed, but the little casket which held the reflections he had had on the banks of the Gran was saved. Thence issued that incomparable book in which Epictetus was surpassed, that gospel of those who have no belief in the supernatural, a gospel which only in our own days has been fully understood. A true and eternal gospel, the book of *Meditations* will never grow old, for it affirms no dogma. The virtue of Marcus Aurelius rests, like our own, upon reason and nature. St. Louis was a very virtuous man because he was a Christian; Marcus Aurelius was the most pious of men, not because he was a pagan, but because he was a perfectly developed man. He was the honour of human nature and not of a determinate religion. Science may come and apparently destroy God and the immortal soul, while the *Meditations* will remain young with life and truth. The religion of Marcus Aurelius is the absolute religion, that resulting from the simple fact of a high moral consciousness confronting the universe. It is of no race and of no country. No revolution, no change, no discovery can ever alter it.

SPINOZA.[1]

On this day, two hundred years ago, in the afternoon about the present hour, there lay dying at the age of forty-three, on the quiet quay of the Pavilioengracht, not far from here, a poor man whose life had been so profoundly silent, that his last sigh was scarcely heard. He had occupied a lonely room in the house of some worthy trades-people who, without understanding him, felt an instinctive veneration for him. On the morning of his last day on earth he went down as usual to join his hosts; there had been religious services that day; the gentle philosopher talked with those honest folk about what the minister had said, and with warm approval advised them to conform to it. The host and hostess (they deserve to be named, for by their honest sincerity they are entitled to a place in this beautiful idyll of the Hague told by Colerus[2]), the Van der Spyks, husband and wife, returned to their devotions. When they reached home again their quiet lodger was dead. His funeral, on the 25th of February, was conducted like that of a Christian believer, in the new church on the Spuy. All the people of the neighbourhood greatly regretted the disappearance of the sage, who had lived amongst them like one of themselves. His hosts kept his memory like a religion, and none of those who had been in his presence ever spoke of

[1] An address delivered at the unveiling of a monument to Spinoza at the Hague, February 21st, 1877.

[2] See Note XXV.

him without calling him, according to usage, "the blessed Spinoza."

About the same time, however, any one capable of examining the current of opinion then setting in among the professedly enlightened circles of the Pharisaism of that time, would have seen, in singular contrast, this philosopher, so deeply loved by the simple and the pure of heart, become the bugbear of the narrow orthodoxy, that pretended to having the monopoly of truth. A scoundrel, a pestilence, an imp of hell, the most wicked atheist that ever lived, a man steeped in crime—this was what the lonely man of the Pavilioengracht grew to be in the opinion of right-thinking theologians and philosophers. Portraits of him were put in circulation, exhibiting him as "bearing on his face signs of reprobation."

But justice was to have her day. The human mind reaching towards the end of the eighteenth century, in Germany especially, a more enlightened theology and a philosophy of wider scope, recognised in Spinoza the precursor of a new gospel. Jacobi[1] took the public into his confidence with regard to a conversation he had had with Lessing. He had gone to Lessing with the hope of enlisting the latter's aid against Spinoza. What was his amazement when he found in Lessing an avowed Spinozist! "Εν καὶ πᾶν," said Lessing to him, "there you have the whole of philosophy." Him whom a whole century had declared to be an atheist, Novalis called a "God-intoxicated man." His forgotten books were published and eagerly sought after. Schleiermacher, Goethe, Hegel, Schelling, all with one voice proclaimed Spinoza the father of modern thought. It may be that there was some exaggeration in this first outburst of tardy reparation; but time, which

[1] See Note XXVI.

assigns to everything its place, has fully ratified Lessing's judgment; and there is not an enlightened mind to-day that does not acknowledge Spinoza as the man who, in his day, possessed the highest consciousness of God. It is with this conviction that you have desired his pure and humble tomb to have its anniversary. It is the common assertion of a free faith in the infinite which brings together on this day, at the spot that witnessed so much virtue, the choicest gathering that a man of genius could have, grouped around him, after his death. A sovereign as distinguished by her intellectual as by her moral gifts is with us in spirit. A prince who can justly appreciate merit of every kind, by lending this solemnity the distinction of his presence, desires to testify that of the glories of Holland there is not one alien to him, and that no lofty thought escapes his enlightened judgment and his philosophic admiration.

I.

The illustrious Baruch de Spinoza was born at Amsterdam, at the time when your republic was attaining the climax of its glory and power. He belonged to that great race which, by the influence it has exercised and the services it has rendered, occupies so exceptional a position in the history of civilisation. In its own way a miracle, the development of the Jewish people takes rank beside that other miracle, the development of the Greek mind; for, if Greece was the first to realise the ideal of poetry, of science, of philosophy, of art, of profane life, the Jewish people—if I may so express myself—created the religion of humanity. Its prophets were the first to proclaim in the world the idea of righteousness, the re-vindication of the rights of the weak—a re-vindication so much the more violent, in that, all idea of future reward being unknown to them, they dreamed of the realisation of their ideal upon the earth in the near future. It was a Jew, Isaiah, who, seven hundred and fifty years before Jesus Christ, dared to affirm that sacrifices are of small importance, and that there is but one thing needful, pure hands and a pure heart. Then, when earthly events seemed to contradict hopelessly those brilliant Utopias, Israel made an unparalleled change of front.

Transporting into the domain of pure idealism that Kingdom of God to which the world could not attain, one half of its children founded Christianity, and the other half breathed through the flaming fagots of the Middle Ages that imperturbable protest. "Hear, O Israel, the Lord thy God is one God; holy is His name." This potent tradition of idealism, of hope against all hope, this religion that obtains the most heroic sacrifices from its adherents, though it be not of its essence to promise them anything certain beyond this life,—such was the healthy and bracing atmosphere in which Spinoza developed. His education was at first entirely Hebraic; the great literature of Israel was his earliest, and indeed his perpetual instructress, the meditation of his whole life.

As generally happens, Hebrew literature, by assuming the character of a sacred book, had become the subject of a conventional exegesis, in which the explanation of the old texts according to the meaning of their authors was of less importance than the discovery in them of nourishment for the moral and religious needs of the time. The penetrating mind of young Spinoza soon discerned the defects of the Synagogue exegesis; the Bible, as it was taught to him, was disfigured by the accumulated misinterpretations of more than two thousand years. He resolved to make his way beyond them. Essentially he was at one with the true fathers of Judaism, in particular with the great Maimonides,[1] who had found a way of introducing into Judaism the most daring philosophical speculations. With marvellous sagacity he foresaw the great results of the critical exegesis which, a hundred and twenty-five years later, was to provide the true signification of the noblest works of the Hebrew genius. Was this to destroy the Bible? Has that admirable literature lost anything by being understood in its true sense, rather than by being relegated outside the common laws of humanity? Certainly not. The truths that science reveals ever surpass the dreams that science dispels. The world of Laplace, I imagine, exceeds in beauty that of a Cosmas Indicopleustes,[2] who pictured the universe to himself as a chest, on the lid of which the stars glide along in grooves at the distance of a few leagues from us. The Bible is in the same way more beautiful, when we have learnt to see therein—ranged in order on the background of a thousand years—each sigh, each aspiration, each prayer of the most exalted religious consciousness that ever existed, than when we force ourselves to regard it as a book unlike any other, written, preserved, and interpreted in direct opposition to all the ordinary rules of the human intellect.

But the mediæval persecutions had the customary effect of persecutions; they had made men's minds narrow and timorous. A few years previously, at Amsterdam, the ill-fated Uriel Acosta[3] had cruelly expiated hesitations in belief that fanaticism finds as culpable as avowed infidelity. Young Spinoza's boldness was received still more unfavourably; he was anathematised, and had to submit to an excommunication which he had not courted. What an old story this is! Religious communions, the beneficent cradles

[1] See Note XXVII. [2] See Note XXVIII.
[3] See Note XXIX.

of so much earnestness and virtue, will hear of no refusal to be imprisoned in their bosom; they lay claim to hold captive for ever the life that has had its beginning within them; they treat as apostasy the legitimate emancipation of the soul that seeks to take its flight alone. It is as though the egg should upbraid, as ungrateful, the bird that escaped from it; the egg was essential at its time,—when it became a bondage it had to be broken.

It was indeed truly wonderful that Erasmus of Rotterdam should have felt his cell to be too narrow for him, that Luther should not have preferred his monkish vows to that vow—holy in a very different sense—which man, by the very fact of his being, contracts with truth! Had Erasmus continued in his monastic routine, or had Luther gone on distributing indulgences, they would have been apostates indeed. Spinoza was the greatest of modern Jews, and Judaism exiled him. Nothing can be more simple; it had to be so, and it must ever be so. Finite symbols, prisons of the infinite spirit, eternally protest against the efforts of idealism to enlarge them. For its part the human spirit struggles everlastingly for more air and more light. Eighteen hundred and fifty years ago the Synagogue denounced, as a false prophet, him who was to give unequalled lustre to the maxims of the Synagogue. And the Christian Church, how often has she not driven forth from her bosom those who should have brought her most honour? Our duty in such cases is fulfilled if we keep in pious memory the education which we received in our childhood. Let the old churches be free to brand with criminality him who leaves them; they will not succeed in receiving from us any other feeling save that of gratitude; for after all, the harm that they can do us is as nothing to the good that they have done.

II.

Here, then, we have the excommunicated one of the Amsterdam Synagogue forced to create a spiritual abode for himself, outside the home which would have no more of him. He had the deepest sympathy with Christianity, but he dreaded all chains, and did not embrace it. Descartes had lately renewed philosophy by his firm and sober rationalism; Descartes was his master. Spinoza took up the problems where that man of great mind had left them, and saw that, through fear of the Sorbonne,[1] his theology had always remained somewhat arid. Oldenburg[2] asked him one day what fault he had to find with the philosophy of Descartes and Bacon; and Spinoza replied that their principal fault consisted in not occupying themselves sufficiently with the First Cause. It may be that his recollections of Jewish theology, that ancient wisdom of the Hebrews before which he often bows, in this matter inspired him with more lofty views, more ambitious yearnings. Not only the ideas of the Deity held by the vulgar, but even those of thinkers, seemed to him inadequate. He clearly saw that we cannot assign a limited part to the infinite, that the divine is either all or is nothing, and that if the divine has reality at all, it must pervade everything. For twenty years he meditated on these problems, without permitting his thoughts to leave them for an instant. Our distaste for systems and abstract formulæ does not allow us nowadays to accept absolutely the propositions in which he thought that he held the secrets of the infinite. The universe for Spinoza, as for Descartes, was only extension and thought; chemistry and physiology were wanting in that great school, which was too exclusively geometrical

[1] See Note XXX. [2] See Note XXXI.

and mechanical. Foreign to the theory of life, and to the ideas as to the composition of matter which chemistry was to reveal, still too much attached to the scholastic terms of *substance* and *attribute*, Spinoza did not attain to that living and fruitful infinite exhibited in the science of nature and history, as presiding in limitless space over a development that ever tends to grow more and more intense. But making allowance for a certain aridity of expression, what grandeur there is in that inflexible geometrical induction leading up to the supreme proposition: "It is of the nature of the substance to develop itself necessarily by an infinity of infinite attributes infinitely modified!" God is thus absolute thought, universal consciousness. The ideal exists —it might even be said that it is the sole existence, and that all the rest is but appearance and frivolity. Bodies and souls are mere *modes*, of which God is the substance; it is only the modes that know duration, the substance is wholly in eternity. In this way God does not prove himself, for his existence results from his idea alone; everything contains and supposes him. God is the condition of all existence and all thought. If God did not exist, thought would be able to conceive more than nature could provide, which is a contradiction.

Spinoza did not clearly see universal progress; the world, as he conceives it, seems, as it were, crystallised in a matter which is incorruptible extension, in a soul which is immutable thought. His feeling for God deprives him of his feeling for man; face to face with the infinite unceasingly, he did not sufficiently perceive that part of the divine which is concealed in relative manifestations. But, better than any other man, he saw the eternal identity which is the basis of all transient evolutions. Whatever is limited seemed to him frivolous, and unworthy to occupy the mind of a philosopher. With daring flight he soared to the lofty snow-covered summits, without casting a glance on the rich display of life blossoming on the mountain-side. At that altitude, where every breast save his pants for breath, he lives, he finds delight, he flourishes as ordinary men do in mild and temperate climes. What is essential for him is the glacier air, keen and strong and penetrating. He does not ask to be followed; he is like Moses, to whom secrets unknown to the multitude of men were revealed upon the high places. Be assured of this, he was the seer of his age; he was the man of his own day who saw most profoundly into God.

III.

It might well be supposed that, all alone as he was upon these snowy peaks, he was in human affairs wrongheaded, or Utopian, or disdainfully sceptical. But that was by no means the case. He never ceased to be preoccupied with the application of his principles to human societies. The pessimism of Hobbes and the dreams of Thomas More were equally repugnant to him. At least one half of the *Theologico-Political Treatise*, which appeared in 1670, might be reprinted to-day without losing any of its cogency. Listen to its admirable title:—*Tractatus Theologico-Politicus continens dissertationes aliquot, quibus ostenditur, libertatem philosophandi non tantum salva pietate et republicæ pace posse concedi, sed eamdem nisi cum pace reipublicæ ipsaque pietate tolli non posse.* For centuries past it had been imagined that society rested upon metaphysical dogmas. Spinoza profoundly saw that these dogmas, assumed to be necessary to humanity, could not escape discussion; that revelation,—if such there be,—traversing, in order to reach us, the faculties of the human mind, is no less than everything else open to criticism. I wish that I could quote in its entirety that admirable Chapter XX., in which the great writer establishes with masterly superiority that dogma, new then, and even now contested, which is called liberty of conscience.

"The final end of the State," he says, "consists not in dominating over men, restraining them by fear, subjecting them to the will of others; but, on the contrary, in preserving intact the natural right of each to live without injury to himself or others. No, I say, the State has not for its end the transformation of men from reasonable beings into animals or automata; it has for end so to act that its citizens should develop soul and body in security, and make free use of their reason. Hence the true end of the State is liberty. Whosoever means to respect the rights of a sovereign should never act in opposition to his decrees; but each has the right to think what he wills, and to say what he thinks, provided he content himself with speaking and teaching in the name of pure reason, and do not attempt on his private authority to introduce innovations into the State. For example, a citizen who demonstrates that a certain law is repugnant to pure reason, and holds that for that cause it ought to be abrogated,—if he submit his opinions to the judgment of the sovereign, to whom alone it belongs to establish and abolish laws, and if meanwhile he act in nowise contrary to law,—that man certainly deserves well of the State as the best of citizens. . . .

"Even if we admit the possibility of so stifling men's liberty, and laying such a yoke upon them that they dare not even whisper without the sovereign's approbation, never most surely can they be prevented from thinking as they will. What then must ensue? That men will think one way and speak another, that consequently good faith—a virtue most necessary to the State—will become corrupted, that adulation—a detestable thing—and perfidy will be had in repute, entailing the decadence of all good and healthy morality. What can be more disastrous to a State than to exile honest citizens as evil-doers, because they do not share the opinions of the crowd, and are ignorant of the art of feigning? What more fatal than to treat as enemies and doom to death, men whose only crime is that of thinking independently? The scaffold which should be the terror of the wicked is thus turned into the glorious theatre, where virtue and toleration shine out in all their lustre, and publicly cover the sovereign majesty with approbrium. Beyond question there is but one thing to be learnt from such a spectacle,—to imitate those noble martyrs; or, if one fears death, to become the cowardly flatterers of power. Nothing, then, is so full of peril as to refer and submit to divine rights matters of pure speculation, and to impose laws on opinions which are, or may be, subjects of discussion amongst men. If the authority of the State limited itself to the repression of actions, while allowing impunity to words, controversies would turn less often into seditions."

Wiser than many so-called practical men, our thinker sees perfectly well that the only durable governments are reasonable governments, and that the only reasonable governments are tolerant governments. Far from absorbing the individual in the State, he grants him solid guarantees against the State's omnipotence. He is not a revolutionary, but a moderate man; he transforms, he explains, but he does not destroy. His God is not of those that take pleasure in sacrifices, in ceremonies, and in the savour of incense; nevertheless, Spinoza is far from having any design to overthrow religion. For Christianity he entertains a profound veneration, a tender and sincere respect. In his doctrine the supernatural is meaningless; according to his principles, anything outside nature would be out of being, and consequently inconceivable. Seers and prophets have been men like others:—

"It is not thinking but dreaming," he says, "to hold that prophets have had a human body and not a human soul, and that consequently their knowledge and sensations have been of a different nature from ours."

"The prophetic faculty has not been the dower of one people alone—the Jews. The quality of Son of God has not been the privilege of one man alone. . . . To state my views openly, I tell you that it is not absolutely necessary to know Christ after the flesh; but it is otherwise when we speak of the Son of God—that is to say, of the eternal Wisdom of God, which has manifested itself in all things, and most fully in the human soul, and above all in Jesus Christ. Without this wisdom none can attain the state of beatitude, since it alone teaches us what is true and what is false, what is right and what is wrong. . . . As to what certain Churches have added . . . I have expressly warned you that I know not what they mean, and, to speak frankly, I may confess that they seem to me to use the same kind of language as they would use, if they spoke of a circle assuming the nature of a square."

Are not these almost the very words used by Schleiermacher, and was not Spinoza, the fellow-founder, with Richard Simon,[1] of Biblical exegesis, at the same time the precursor of those liberal theologians who, in our own day, have shown that Christianity can retain all its glory without supernaturalism? His letters to Oldenburg on the

[1] See Note XXXII.

resurrection of Jesus Christ, and of the sense in which St. Paul understood it, are masterpieces which a hundred years later would have served as the manifesto of a whole school of critical theology.

In the eyes of Spinoza it matters little whether mysteries be understood this way or that, provided they be understood in a pious sense; religion has but one end—piety. And to religion we should appeal not for metaphysics, but for practical guidance. At bottom there is but one thing in Scripture as in all revelation, "Love thy neighbour." The fruit of religion is blessedness, and each man participates in it according to his capacity and his efforts. The souls that reason governs—the philosophic souls that even in this world have their life in God—are safe from death. That which death takes from them is worthless; but weak or passionate souls almost wholly perish, and death, instead of being for them a simple accident, involves the very foundation of their being. The ignorant man who allows himself to be guided by blind passion is moved, in a thousand different senses, by external causes, and never enjoys true peace of soul; for him, ceasing to suffer implies ceasing to be. The soul of the sage, on the contrary, can scarcely be disturbed. Possessing by a sort of eternal necessity, consciousness of himself, and of God, and of the world around, he never ceases to be, and ever keeps true peace of soul.

Spinoza could not endure his system to be considered irreligious or subversive. The timid Oldenburg did not conceal from him the fact that some of his opinions seemed, to certain readers, to tend to the overthrow of piety. "Whatever accords with reason," was Spinoza's reply, "is in my belief perfectly favourable to the practice of virtue." The pretended superiority of coarsely positive conceptions in the matter of religion and the future life found him intractable. "Is it, I ask, to throw off all religion," he said, "to recognise in God the Supreme Good, and thence to conclude that he must be loved with a free soul? To maintain that all our happiness and our most perfect freedom consists in that love, that the reward of virtue is virtue itself, and that a blind and impotent soul finds its punishment in its blindness—is that a denial of all religion?" At the root of all such attacks he saw meanness of soul. According to him, any one who chafed at a disinterested religion, tacitly avowed that reason and virtue had no attraction in his eyes, and that his happiness would lie in living as his passions commanded, did not fear restrain him. "Thus then," he would add, "such an one only abstains from evil, and obeys the divine commandments regretfully, as a slave might do; and, as a recompense for this slavery, he expects from God rewards, which in his eyes have infinitely more value than divine love. The more aversion and remoteness from righteousness he may have felt, the more he hopes to be recompensed; and he imagines that those who are not restrained by the same fear as himself do what he would fain do, that is to say, live lawlessly." Spinoza held, with justification, that this manner of seeking to gain Heaven, by doing precisely what is requisite to merit Hell, was contrary to reason, and that there was something absurd in pretending to gain God's favour and avowing at the same time to him, that without dread, one would not love him.

IV.

He felt the danger of touching beliefs, in which few persons admit these subtle distinctions. *Caute* was his favourite motto; and his friends having made him aware of the explosion that the *Ethica* would be certain to produce, he kept it unpublished until his death. He had no literary vanity, nor did he seek renown—possibly indeed because he was sure of having it without seeking. He was perfectly happy; so he has told us, and let us take him at his word. He has done better still: he has bequeathed his secret to us. Listen to the recipe of the "Prince of Atheists" for the discovery of happiness. It is the love of God. To love God is to live in God. Life in God is the best and the most perfect life, because it is the most reasonable, the happiest, the fullest; in a word, because it gives us more *being* than any other life, and most completely satisfies the fundamental desire which constitutes our essence.

His practical life was entirely regulated by these maxims; it was a masterpiece of good sense and judgment. It was governed with the profound skill of the wise man who wishes one thing alone and always ends by obtaining it. Never did policy so well combine end and means. Had he been less reserved he might perhaps have met the fate of the unfortunate Acosta. Since he loved truth for truth's sake, he was indifferent to the abuse which his constancy in speaking it brought down upon him; he did not utter a word in reply to the attacks of which he was the object. He himself never attacked any one. "It is contrary to my habits," he used to say, "to seek to discover the errors into which other men have fallen." Had he chosen to be an official personage, his life would have been filled with persecution, or at least disgrace. He was nothing, and desired to be nothing. *Ama nesciri* was his motto, as it was that of the author of the *Imitation*. He sacrificed all to the peace of his thought; and in doing so he was not egoistical, for his thought was of import to all. He more than once repulsed the wealth that was coming to him, and desired to have only what was absolutely necessary. The King of France offered him a pension, and he declined it with thanks; the Elector Palatine offered him a professorial chair at Heidelburg. "Your liberty will be complete," he was told, "for the prince is convinced that you will not abuse it by disturbing the established religion." "I do not altogether understand within what limits it will be necessary to confine this liberty to philosophise, granted me on condition that I do not disturb the established religion; and besides, the instruction I should give to youth would prevent me from making any personal advance in philosophy. I have only succeeded in procuring a tranquil life by renouncing every kind of public teaching." He felt it to be his duty to think; in fact he did the thinking of mankind, whose ideas he anticipated by more than a hundred years.

This same instinctive sagacity he carried into all the relations of life; he felt that public opinion never allows a man two forms of daring at once; and so, being a freethinker, he thought himself constrained to live like a saint. But I do not phrase the matter well: was not this gentle and pure life the direct expression of his peaceful and loving spirit? The atheist was in those days pictured as a ruffian armed with daggers. Spinoza throughout his whole life was humble, gentle, and pious. His adversaries were naïve enough to take it in ill part; they would fain have had him live according to the conventional model, traversing his life like a demon incarnate, and ending it in despair. Spinoza smiled at this singular pretension, and declined to change his manner of living to please his enemies.

He had excellent friends, was courageous when courage was needed, and protested against popular indignation whenever it appeared to him unjust. Much disillusionment failed to shake him in his fidelity to the Republican party; the liberalism of his opinions was never at the mercy of circumstance. What perhaps did him the most honour was the esteem and sincere affection of the simple folk who lived around him. There is nothing that is worth so much as the esteem of the humble and meek; their judgment is nearly always that of God. For the good Van der Spyks he was evidently the ideal of the perfect lodger. "No one ever gave less trouble," some years after his death they told Colerus. "When he was at home he inconvenienced nobody, passing the best part of his time quietly in his own room. If he happened to tire himself by too prolonged meditation, he would come downstairs and speak to the family about all the topics of ordinary conversation, even about the merest trifles." In fact, there never was seen so affable a neighbour. He often conversed with his hostess, especially at the time of her confinements, and with the rest of the household when any sorrow or sickness befell them. He used to bid the children go to divine service, and, when they returned from the sermon, ask how much they remembered of it. He nearly always strongly supported what the preacher had said. One of the persons whom he most esteemed was Pastor Cordes, an excellent man and a good expounder of the Scriptures. He sometimes went to hear him, and he used to advise his host never to miss the preaching of so able a man. One day his hostess asked him whether he thought she could be saved in the religion she professed. "Your religion is a good one," he replied; "you should not seek after another, nor should you doubt that yours will give you salvation, provided that, attaching yourself to piety, you at the same time live a peaceful and tranquil life." His temperance and good management were admirable. His daily needs were provided for by a handicraft in which he attained great skill—that of polishing lenses. The Van der Spyks handed over to Colerus the little papers in which he used to note his expenses; they averaged about twopence farthing a day. He was very careful to settle his accounts every quarter, so as neither to spend more nor less than his income. His dress was simple, almost poor, but his person radiated forth a tranquil serenity. It was clear that he had found the doctrine that gave him perfect satisfaction.

He was never depressed and never elated; the equability of his humour seems marvellous. Perhaps he felt a little sadness on the day when the daughter of Van den Ende, his professor, preferred Kerkering to him; but I imagine that he speedily consoled himself. "Reason is my delight," he said, "and the end to which in this life I aspire; it means joy and serenity." He objected to any praise of melancholy.

"It is superstition," he maintained, "that sets up sorrow as good, and all that tends to gladness as evil. God would show himself envious were he to take pleasure in my impotence and in the ills I suffer. Rather, in proportion to the greatness of our joy do we reach a higher perfection and participate more fully in the divine nature. . . Joy, therefore, can never be evil so long as it be regulated by the law of our true utility. A virtuous life is not a sad and gloomy one, a life of privation and austerity. How should the Divine Being take delight in the spectacle of my weakness, or impute to me, as meritorious, tears, sobs, terrors—all signs of an impotent soul? Yes," he added emphatically, "it is the part of a wise man to use the things of this life and enjoy them as much as possible; to recruit himself by a temperate and appetising diet; to charm his senses with the perfume and the brilliant verdure of plants; even to adorn his attire, to enjoy music, games, spectacles, and all the amusements that a man can bestow upon himself without detriment to himself." Men do not cease to talk about repentance, humility, and death; but repentance is not a virtue, it is the result of a weakness. Nor is humility one, for it is born in man from his idea of his own inferiority. As for the thought of death, it is the daughter of fear, and only in feeble souls takes up abode. "The one thing of all others," he said, "about which a free man thinks least is death. Wisdom lies in the contemplation not of death but of life."

V.

Since the days of Epictetus and Marcus Aurelius no life had been witnessed so profoundly penetrated by the feeling of the divine. In the twelfth, the thirteenth, and the sixteenth centuries rationalistic philosophy had counted among its adherents very great men, but no saints. Often there had been something repulsive and harsh even in the finest characters among the Italian free-thinkers. Religion had been wholly absent from those lives, not less in revolt against human than against divine laws, of which the last example was that of poor Vanini.[1] Here, on the other hand, we have religion producing free-thought as a part of piety. Religion in such a system is not part of life, it is life itself. What is of importance is not to be in possession of some more or less correct metaphysical phrase, it is to give life an indubitable pole, a supreme direction—the ideal.

It was in so doing that your illustrious compatriot raised aloft a banner that to this day serves to shelter beneath it all

[1] See Note XXXIII.

who think and feel nobly. Yes, religion is eternal; it responds as well to the primary need of the primitive man as to that of the civilised man. It will only perish with humanity itself, or rather, its disappearance would be the proof that degenerate humanity was about to return into the animality whence it emerged. And yet no dogma, no worship, no formula can, in these days of ours, adequately express the religious sentiment. We must allow these two apparently contradictory statements to stand confronting one another. Woe to him who asserts that the era of religions is past! Woe to him who deems it possible to give back to the old symbols the force they possessed when they leant upon the imperturbable dogmatism of other days! With this dogmatism we must needs dispense; we must dispense with the fixed beliefs which have been the sources of so much strife and division, and also of so much fervent conviction; we must cease to believe that it is our duty to keep others in beliefs which we no longer share. Spinoza was right in his horror of hypocrisy: hypocrisy is cowardly and dishonest, but above all it is useless. In truth who is deceived here? The persistence of the upper classes in unreservedly patronising the religious forms of other days in the sight of the uncultured classes, will have but one effect—that of ruining their own authority at those times of crisis when it is desirable that the people should still cherish a belief in the reason and virtue of the few.

Honour then to Spinoza, who dared to say: Reason before all; reason cannot be contrary to the interests of humanity, if we only understand what these interests really are. But let us remind those who are carried away by unreflecting impatience, that Spinoza never conceived religious revolution being aught else than a transformation of formulæ. What was for him essential continued to exist under other terms. If, on the one hand, he energetically repudiated the theocratic power of a clergy conceived as being distinct from civil society, and the tendency of the State to meddle with metaphysical questions, he never, on the other hand, disowned either the State or religion. He wished the State to be tolerant, and religion free. We desire nothing more. We cannot impose on others beliefs which we do not hold ourselves. When the believers of other days became persecutors, they showed themselves to be tyrannical; but they were at least consistent. Were we to do as they did, we should be simply absurd. Our religion is a feeling which may be garbed in many forms. These forms are far from being all of equal value; but there is not one of them that has strength or authority to exclude the others. Liberty,—this is the last word of Spinoza's religious politics. Let it be the last word of our own! It is the most honest part to take; and at the same time it is perhaps the most efficacious and certain as regards the progress of civilisation.

Humanity, in fact, advances along the path of progress with prodigiously unequal steps. The rude and violent Esau is impatient at the slow pace of Jacob's flock. Let us allow time to all. Let us assuredly not permit simplicity and ignorance to fetter the free movements of the intellect; but, on the other hand, do not let us disturb the slow evolution of less active minds. The liberty of some to be absurd is the condition of the liberty of others to be reasonable. Services to the human spirit rendered by violence are not services at all. That those who do not take truth seriously should exercise constraint to obtain outward submission,—what can be more natural? But we who believe that truth is something real and deserving of supreme respect, how can we dream of obtaining by force an adhesion, valueless when it is not the fruit of free conviction? We no longer admit sacramental formulæ, operating by their own virtue independently of the intelligence of him to whom they are applied. For us a belief has only value when it has been gained by the reflection of the individual, when it is by him understood, by him assimilated. A mental conviction caused by higher authority is as perfect a piece of nonsense as a love that is won by force, or a commanded sympathy. Let us promise ourselves that not only shall we ever defend our freedom against all that would fain assail it, but also that, if the need arises, we shall defend the freedom of those who have not always respected ours, and who probably would not respect it if they were the masters now.

It was Holland that had the glory, more than two hundred years ago, of demonstrating the possibility of these theories by realising them.

"Must we prove," said Spinoza, "that this freedom of thought gives rise to no serious inconvenience, and that it is competent to keep men, openly diverse in their opinions, reciprocally respectful of each other's rights? Examples abound, and we need not go far to seek them. Let us instance the town of Amsterdam, whose considerable growth—an object of admiration for other nations—is simply the fruit of this freedom. In the midst of this flourishing republic, this great city, men of all nations and all sects live together in the most perfect harmony; . . . and there is no sect, however odious, whose members, provided they do not offend against the rights of any man, may not publicly find aid and protection before the magistrates."

Descartes was of the same opinion when he came and asked of your country the tranquillity which was essential to his thought. Then, thanks to the noble privilege of a free country, so gloriously maintained by your fathers against all foes, this land of Holland became the place of refuge in which the human intellect, sheltered from the tyrannies which overspread Europe, found air to breathe, a public to understand it, and organs wherein to multiply its voice —elsewhere gagged and silent.

Deep indeed are the sufferings of our age, and cruel are its perplexities. We cannot with impunity raise so many problems before we possess the elements to resolve them. It is not we who have shattered that crystal Paradise with its silver and azure gleams, by which so many eyes have been charmed to consolation. But it lies in fragments. What is shattered is shattered; and never will an earnest spirit undertake the puerile task of restoring ignorance that has once been destroyed, or of giving new life to dispelled illusions. The populations of great towns have almost everywhere ceased to believe in the supernatural; were we to sacrifice our convictions and sincerity in an attempt to give their faith back to them, we should not succeed. And besides, the supernatural, as once it was understood, is not the ideal.

The cause of the supernatural is compromised, the cause of the ideal is unscathed; and so it will ever be. The ideal remains the soul of the world, the permanent God, the primordial, efficient, and final Cause of the universe. This is the basis of eternal religion. In order to adore God we need no more than Spinoza miracles or self-interested prayers. So long as there be in the human heart one fibre to vibrate at the sound of that which is true, and just, and honourable, so long as the instinctively pure soul prefers purity to life, so long as there be found friends of truth ready to sacrifice their peace in the cause of science, friends of righteousness to devote themselves to holy and useful works of mercy, womanly hearts to love whatever is good, beautiful, and pure, artists to render it by sound, and colour, and words of inspiration,—so long God will dwell within us. It could only be when egoism, meanness of soul, narrowness of mind, indifference to knowledge, contempt for human rights, forgetfulness of that which is great and noble, invaded the world,—it could only be then that God would be in humanity no more. But far from us be thoughts like these! Our aspirations, our sufferings, our very faults and temerities, are the proof that the ideal lives in us. Yes, human life is still something divine! Our apparent negations are often nothing more than the scruples of timid minds that fear to pass beyond the limits of their knowledge. They are a worthier homage to the Divinity than the hypocritical adoration of a spirit given over to routine. God is still within us! *Est Deus in nobis.*

Let us all unite in bending before the great and illustrious thinker who, two centuries ago, proved better than any other man, both by the example of his life and by the power—still fresh and young—of his works, how much spiritual joy and holy unction there is in thoughts like these. Let us with Schleiermacher offer the most exquisite words of homage of which we are capable to the shades of the holy and misunderstood Spinoza.

"The sublime spirit of the world penetrated him; the infinite was his beginning and his end; the universal his only and eternal love. Living in holy innocence and profound humility, he contemplated himself in the world of eternity, and saw that he too was for that world a mirror worthy of love. He was full of religion and full of the Holy Spirit; and therefore he appears to us alone and unequalled; a master in his art, but lifted above the profane, without disciples and without right of citizenship anywhere."

That right of citizenship you are now about to confer upon him. Your monument will be the connecting link between his genius and the earth. His soul will brood like a good angel over the spot where his short journey among men came to an end. Woe to him who, passing by, should dare to level an insult at that sweet and pensive figure! He would be punished as all vulgar hearts are punished—by his very vulgarity and powerlessness to comprehend the divine. Meanwhile, from his granite pedestal Spinoza will teach to all the way of happiness that he himself found, and for ages to come the cultivated man who passes along the Pavilioengracht will inwardly say: "It is perhaps in this place that God has been felt most closely."

HENRI-FRÉDÉRIC AMIEL.

AN infinite gratitude is due to the persons who, animated by a sentiment of pious friendship, have undertaken the difficult task of introducing Henri-Frédéric Amiel to a public with which that distinguished thinker preoccupied himself much, but which a certain timidity prevented him from addressing directly. Amiel's intellectual position is one of the most peculiar of our time; his life exhibits admirably some of the maladies that prey upon our generation. With philosophical abilities of a high order, Amiel only reached melancholy; possessed of true literary qualities, he could not give to his ideas the form which they demanded. A perfectly sincere man, he failed to have a steadfast design in the direction of his life. Moralists and public men of a lesser order have made greater mark than he; writers a hundred times less learned have left deeper traces in our literary history; a multitude of mediocre natures have perhaps rendered more service to the cause of truth and goodness than this passionate lover of the ideal.

Had Amiel been of the band, assuredly the best among the elect, that has taken for its motto *Ama nesciri*, there were nothing more to say. It is an accepted opinion with experienced critics that literature diminishes what it touches, that the finest shades of feeling will be for ever unknown, that the truest and most powerful ideas that men have had in the universe have remained unwritten, or rather unexpressed. God and his angels, as people used to say, have had the privilege of beholding the only perfect manifestations of moral and intellectual order; that is, of meditations and feelings, evolving themselves in the midst of an absolute objectivity, untainted by the underlying thought of their possible employment. The man of silent virtue, the great heart that makes no parade of its heroism, the noble mind that only delivers, as it were by compulsion, its exalted views, are superior to the mere craftsman in words, preoccupied with giving a form to opinions which, with him, are not perhaps very profound. Amiel, although a very virtuous man, had not reached the height of disinterestedness of those ascetics, who vow themselves to an everlasting silence. He was not exempt from the great literary evil, the false idea, that thought and sentiment exist to be expressed, the idea that makes men turn from loving life for its own sake, and attributes an exaggerated value to mere talent. Amiel desires to produce, but he cannot help feeling all the time that he is not a man of letters. To use a vulgar phrase which a certain species of literature has put into fashion, he is a *raté*, because he does not know how to win the public to the order of ideas of his choice; but he is a *raté* who is aware of what is wanting in him, who worships what he does not possess, and wastes himself with regret. He does not see sufficiently that without being a great writer, one can do things of the first importance; and then he has recourse to the falsest of compromises—the *journal intime*, disconnected thoughts, memoirs destined for their writer's eyes alone.

That is a dangerous, sometimes unhealthy literary habit, a habit generally indulged in by those who have none other; and upon which, save in exceptional cases, must rest *a priori* a certain condemnation. The man who finds sufficient time to write a *journal intime* does not appear to us to have fully grasped how vast the world is. The volume of knowledge to be acquired is immense. The history of humanity is scarcely commenced upon; the study of nature holds in store discoveries we cannot possibly foresee. How, in the presence of such a colossal task as this, can we stop to feast upon ourselves, to doubt life itself? Far better would it be to take up the spade and toil. The day when we can permit ourselves to loiter behind in the diversion of a discouraged mind, will be the day when we begin to see that knowledge has its limits. But even supposing that in the ages we may perceive such bounds for history, we shall never perceive them for nature. Even the problems that appear wholly insoluble, such as those of physical astronomy, are susceptible of a sudden transformation, altogether unforeseen. Working upon formulæ more and more comprehensive, acquired by past scientific generations, physics, chemistry, and biology have before them a future which ever widens as we advance. My friend, M. Berthelot, would be able to find occupation during hundreds of consecutive lives without ever writing about himself. I estimate that I should require five hundred years to exhaust the domain of Semitic studies, as I understand them; and if ever my taste for them should begin to grow enfeebled, I should learn Chinese. That new world, as yet almost untouched by criticism, would keep me in appetite for an indefinite time. Subjective scepticism, doubt concerning the legitimacy of our faculties—such is the snare in which are caught natures attacked by the malady of over-scrupulousness. Apprehensions of this kind invariably come from a certain indolence of mind. He that has a thirst for reality is dragged out of himself. Thus it is that a man of genius like Victor Hugo has never had leisure for introspection. When one is powerfully attracted by things one is sure that they exist, and that one is not grasping a vain phantasmagoria.

Amiel has not that love of the universe that gives us eyes for it alone. For more than thirty years he did not let a day pass without observing and describing his state of mind; and he consigned his reflections to quarto note-books which, brought together, form a total of sixteen thousand pages. *Felix Culpa!* Out of this indigestible mass Amiel's friends (ah, what a good thing it is to leave true friends behind one!) have collected two volumes of *pensées*, which offer us, without any sacrifice being made to art, the perfect reflection of a singularly honest modern mind, which had arrived at the highest degree of culture; and at the same time a finished picture of the sufferings of a sterile genius. These two volumes certainly hold a place among the most interesting philosophical writings that have appeared during the last few years.

As a matter of fact, Amiel's deficiencies are as pronounced as they well could be. He himself takes a pleasure in emphasising them, and putting them in the foreground; but there is not one amongst them that does not arise from an excess of nobility and high principle. "I sever myself obstinately from doing anything that might give me pleasure, serve me, or help me. My passion is to do hurt to my own interests, to defy common sense, to be possessed with a zeal for my own detriment. . . . I am ashamed of my own interests, as of an ignoble and servile cause."

"What a singular nature is mine," he cries, "and what a *bizarre* tendency!—not to dare to enjoy anything frankly and without scruple; and to feel forced to leave the table for fear the feast should come to an end." "So soon as a thing attracts me," he says again, "I turn away my head from it, or rather, I can neither content myself with the unsatisfying, nor find anything that can satisfy my aspirations. The Real disgusts me, and I cannot find the Ideal." That is true. His want of power is due to his ultra-perfection. "In love," says M. Scherer, "he shrank from an avowal, in literature he shrank from the production of a book." The man of letters is never without some failing, or rather, the very profession of letters is a failing. The perfect man of Amiel's dream would not have talent; talent is a frivolous vice, from which, before all else, a saint must mortify himself.

Amiel's sterility has another origin—the too great diversity of his intellectual and ethical basis. Variety in this respect is excellent; but the elements should not neutralise one another. One amongst them must dominate, and the others be only accessory. Amiel is too much of a hybrid to be fertile. The excellent German education which he received was ever at variance with the other parts of his nature. He laid the blame on the language; he believed that French was the cause of the difficulty that he experienced in giving form to his thoughts. It was a profound mistake. "The French language," he says, "cannot express origin or germination; it depicts effects, results, the *caput mortuum*, but not cause, movement, energy, the growth of some phenomenon, whatever it may be. It is analytical and descriptive; but it does not assist comprehension, for it fails to give a glimpse of the beginnings and developments of anything." Had Amiel possessed a better knowledge of the language that he habitually wrote, he would have recognised that French suffices for the expression of all thought, even of the thought most alien to its ancient spirit; and that, if in the transfusion it lets certain details drop out of sight, these details are simply the superfluities which hinder the new thought from taking upon itself the garment of universality. Amiel was not a perfect master of his instrument. Ignorant of some of its notes, he judged it incapable of rendering certain sounds, and then in impatience he strained it. He had done better in studying it more thoroughly.

While he was young, and nearly at the age for leaving college, Amiel went to Germany. He embraced the intellectual discipline, then dominant, with much ardour. The Hegelian school taught him its complicated system of thought, and at the same blow rendered him incapable of writing. This school laid greater emphasis on loquacity, and dissertations upon all kinds of subjects, than on the ordered composition exacted by prose. Hegel has his good points, but it is necessary to know how to take him. He must be limited to an infusion; he makes an excellent tea, but to munch the dry leaves is undesirable. Amiel did this too much. Everything becomes for him a matter of system, so much so in fact, that when one day he meets a very pretty girl in the Jura, in the neighbourhood of Soleure, he passes his day in constructing a theory of flirtation, and the disadvantages of beauty. Had only his Hegelian training given him the scientific spirit! But it did nothing of the kind. No school of thought has spread abroad more ingenious or more profound ideas than that of Hegel. But in scarcely any direction has it produced true men of science. Hegel was a little akin to Raymond Lully,[1] that is to say, he cherished the delusive idea that logical machinery and general processes can take the place of the direct study of realities. From this ensued a species of lassitude, which very quickly manifested itself in the

[1] See Note XXXIV.

leaders and adepts of this school, in other respects so eminent. There can be no curiosity when the result is seen in advance. The end after which one is striving with the tourniquets of logic is quickly discerned; but the end of reality never comes in sight.

This ill-harmonised education is the cause of the species of slanting foundation that renders the structure of Amiel's life so unstable. He is not firmly established in his chair. He has not a sufficiently clear conception of the ultimate goal of the human mind, of that which gives a serious foundation to life. He is neither a *savant* nor a scholar. More than once he reiterates the declaration that for him the supreme ideal is scholarship; but he feels strongly that in him this art is wanting. He is even led into a false conception. He discriminates too much between substance and form; he would willingly believe that writing is a thing apart from thinking. He is one of the most sincere seekers after truth who have ever lived, he is nearly a saint; and yet, despite all that, he halts at every turning of the road to weep over imaginary troubles, or (and this is still more singular) over imaginary sins, and to remark upon details that he who presses on never stops to notice. He himself is never in a hurry. That perhaps is a good quality; but it is the mark of a mind only moderately possessed with curiosity, with the thirst for realities. He does not picture the world to himself as either so great or so wonderful as it really is. He would willingly imagine (Heaven pardon me!) that the last word can be said about it. But that is not so. All remains to be achieved, or re-achieved, in the province of the sciences of nature and humanity. When one is conscious of working at that infinite task, one has no time to stop for melancholy reflections on the way.

What is most vexatious is, that this highly-strung philosophy did not give him the happiness he deserved. At a first glance it is difficult to see what grievance he had to allege against destiny. He was born particularly well endowed both intellectually and morally; he had all the means of acquiring a high culture; he had never to struggle against very hard necessities; he lived for sixty years, suffering much it is true in later life, but always with intellectual powers untrammelled. With all these advantages, it seems as though he ought to have been as happy as a king; and yet the habitual trend of his thought is an outcry against fate. It appears that his childhood was not surrounded with affection; and that is one of the worst things that can happen to a man. The joys and sorrows of early years reflect themselves on our whole life. For another thing, Geneva was evidently one of the places in the world least suited to his nature. His German education had, as it were, made him a stranger to it; and then a little state is not unlike a little town. It is possible that Amiel did not observe a system of precautions sufficiently elaborate for the eyes of his neighbours. When one is not as other men are, one must, to a certain extent, keep aloof from them. No one of us has the right of exacting more than simple toleration from the society of which he forms a part. It is nearly always by kindly and just dealing that one succeeds therein. It was part of Amiel's ingenuousness to believe himself bound to take part in battles of pygmies, and to make common cause with men who, had he really been one of them, would have understood him no better than the democratic party. In the most disinterested way, he gaily became a reactionary. The man who has vowed his life to the search after truth, and the pursuit of the good, ought not to ally himself absolutely with any of the revolutions which succeed one another in this world. One interest alone he should recognise—that of the human soul and the human mind.

It is greatly to be regretted that Amiel did not come to Paris in 1860, at the time of the founding of the *Revue Germanique.* M. Scherer invited him, M. Sainte-Beuve would have exercised upon him a dominating influence. We should have succeeded, I believe, in diminishing, to his happiness, the malignant action of the ferments of sadness, with which nature, in his first as well as in his second education, had infected him.

Religion, it must be said, had deepened the gravity of the evil. Here assuredly is the most singular side of Amiel's character. This extreme Hegelian, this Buddhist, this rationalist perfectly convinced of the non-existence of the positively supernatural, followed the common creed. Traces of the preaching of Saint-Pierre of Geneva are frequently to be found in his *pensées.* Amiel is not simply a Protestant, he is an orthodox Protestant, very much opposed to liberal Protestantism. He speaks of sin, salvation, redemption, conversion, as though they were realities. It is, above all else, sin that preoccupies him, saddens him,—him the best of men, who less than any one could know what it is. He reproaches me strongly for not taking it sufficiently into account, and he asks two or three times: "What does M. Renan make of sin?" The fact is, as I was saying in my native town the other day, I believe that I simply ignore it. There is the striking difference between Catholic education and Protestant education. Those who, like myself, have received a Catholic education have retained deep traces of it. But these traces are not dogmas, they are dreams. Once that great curtain of cloth of gold, embroidered with silk and cotton and calico, with which Catholicism hides the world from our sight,—once,

I say, this curtain is rent in twain, we see the universe in its infinite splendour, nature in her high and generous majesty. The most emancipated Protestant often retains some touch of melancholy, a depth of intellectual austerity, analogous to Slavonic pessimism. One thing it is to smile at the legend of some mythological saint; it is another to keep the imprint of those terrible mysteries which have brought sadness to so many of the noblest spirits. What is in fact so singular, is that it is the souls least open to sin which torment themselves about it the most, seek for it persistently, and under pretext of ridding themselves of evil that they do not possess, are continually dissecting and tearing themselves open with strokes of the scalpel.

There was besides in Amiel's religious attitude something more than memories of childhood. Those elegant *tours-de-force* which permit him to deny all in speculation, and to affirm all in practice, he must have learned in Berlin from old Marheineke,[1] or from one of his disciples. Since him, the art has only grown, and become more elaborate. The strangest intellectual paradox with which philosophical Germany has ever astonished us, is the curious pretension of a certain school to found religion upon the postulate of pessimism. Have we not lately seen M. Hartmann—that same M. Hartmann who declares flatly that creation is a mistake, and that the hypothesis of not-being would have been far preferable to the hypothesis of being—discover at the same time that religion is necessary, and that it has for its base the inherent evil of human nature?

"Religion," writes M. Hartmann, "has its origin in the fact that the human spirit is continually encountering evil and sin; and that in consequence it strives to explain them, and as far as possible to overcome them. He that asks

[1] See Note XXXV.

himself: 'How can I bring myself to bear with evil; how shall I succeed in reconciling with itself my tormented conscience?'—he is on the path of religion. Whether the stress be laid upon evil or upon sin, it is always discontent with the world that leads to religion. If the painful impressions caused by evil and sin do not weigh sufficiently in the balance to overpower, in a lasting manner, the agreeable impressions of the life of the world, religious enthusiasms of the soul will only be fleeting. It is only when doubt, bitter relatively to the evil, and the anguish of moral guilt have dominated worldly satisfactions, and formed the general current of existence; it is only when the pessimistic feeling has got the upper hand; that religion can be durably established in the soul. Where this pessimistic tendency of mind is not to be found, there religion cannot increase, at least spontaneously."

This is the very antithesis of our ideas. What we think is that a man is religious when he feels satisfied with God and himself. And now, forsooth, we are told that we are only religious when we are in an ill humour and have committed sins! . . . That passes my understanding altogether. More and more as time goes on I feel myself disgusted with the transcendental; and I am coming to believe that the French solution, summing itself up in liberty, and the gradual but inevitable separation of religion and the state, is, in the present position of the human spirit, the only reasonable solution. It is quite true that liberalism has no finality; but it is precisely in that respect that it is right, or at least it is in that respect that it is the only practical expedient, in presence of the individualism in belief, which has become the law of our time.

Lofty minds have often to beware of these reactionary tendencies, masked under the appearance of profound philosophy. Soaring high into the region of the atmosphere, where ideas come into being, and where the great air-currents that bear them spring up, they imagine that they can harness the clouds at their pleasure, and, like Æolus, make the wind blow whither they will. This fine aerial strategy has something pathetic in it, but is at the same time slightly pretentious. They desire to play the part of the lance, that at once strikes and cures. After they have cut away in the most accomplished fashion the root of moral and religious belief, they wish to appear in the guise of the healer; after the reader has passed through the terrors of scepticism, he finds that by the grace of God all is safe. And on this subject I cannot help recalling our eminent thinker, M. Lachelier,[1] the inventor of the most amazing philosophical right-about-face since Kant. After having applied to all the operations of the mind a criticism so corrosive that scarcely anything remains intact, after having made his way to the last extreme of nihilism, he wheels round. One mournful thought suffices to make him find himself to be a perfect Christian. This reconstruction of Christianity on the basis of pessimism is one of the most striking intellectual symptoms of our time. It is so hard to deprive ourselves of the support of an established creed, that after destroying churches built of granite, we build them anew in stucco. That reminds me of the church at Ferney, now serving as a hay-loft, with the inscription, *Deo erexit Voltaire.*

It is a very remarkable fact that the elements of this pessimistic Christianity, by which it is believed possible to replant Christianity in the world, are exclusively drawn from St. Paul. Jesus and Galilean preaching are forgotten; no longer are we under the influence of direct light from

[1] See Note XXXVI.

the sun of the Kingdom of Heaven. I must confess that the dogma of original sin is the one for which I have the least taste. There is no other dogma built so much as this one on the point of a needle. The story of Adam's transgression is only to be found in one of the versions, the alternating pages of which form the tissue of Genesis. Had the Elohistic narrative alone come down to us, we should have heard nothing of original sin. The Jahvistic narrative of the fall of man, otherwise a very beautiful history, and of comparatively great antiquity, was never of much account among the ancient people of Israel. It was St. Paul who first drew from it the frightful dogma that during the centuries has filled humanity with sorrows and terrors. That it was powerful in its time, that Protestantism in particular, whose duty it was to sweep away refuse still more objectionable and gross, may have been justified in accentuating those austere beliefs, which, placing man in a state of absolute dependence on God and Jesus Christ, took him out of the hands of the priest and the official church,—all this is perfectly true; but why should rational beings such as we keep up fictions of this kind? If we are to admit the supernatural element implied in original sin and in redemption, I do not see why we should stop there. The question is one of knowing whether the supernatural exists. When we recognise its existence, we cannot reasonably bargain about the quantity.

Has this dogma of sin at least had the advantage of accounting, in a more or less symbolical way, for the great facts of human history and society? No, assuredly not. Do you wish to tell me that physical and moral evil is all too abundant, that man only attains his end, which is the realisation of a society to a certain extent just, by continuous effort? Oh, that is true, no doubt. But it is giving a mythical and inexact turn to the expression of an evident fact. To us the world reveals, with a total absence of preconceived design, a spontaneous effort, like that of the embryo, towards life and consciousness. The world, or, to be more precise, the planet on which we live, draws, or will draw, from the capital bestowed upon it the *summum* of that which is possible. It needs time for that; but indefinite time is at its disposal. To ask of the universe, and of each of the bodies which compose it, the immediate realisation of absolute perfection, is to demand a flagrant contradiction. Righteousness is achieved by the obscure conscience of the universe, only by means of a certain amount of evil. To be or not to be—that is the choice. But from the moment when the universe has taken—and I believe that it has done well in doing so—the part of being and knowing, the compensating dose of evil is absolutely inevitable.

The metamorphosis of animals is a paroxysm of pain. Pain is the perpetual admonition of life, the incitement to all progress. Why does the insect strive to rid itself of an organ that would impede its new life? Because it suffers. Why does the engendered being desire separation from the engendering being? Because it suffers. Pain creates the effort; it is salutary. It is evident that man is the most highly developed being that we can know. His astonishing prerogatives are purchased on hard conditions. The development of an organism so complicated as the human body implies a considerable amount of suffering. It is impossible for the child not to suffer, for the mother not to suffer, for the old man not to suffer; and as for death, it is the absolutely necessary consequence of the evident law that every organism which has come into existence must one day have an end.

"In sorrow thou shalt bring forth children" is presented

by the theologians as a condemnation following upon a crime; but for that to be exact, it would be necessary that the actually existing period should have been preceded by one in which the woman bore her children painlessly; and that has never been the case, except, it may be, among the lowest races of mankind. The highly-civilised man represents a high-water mark, a maximum obtained by skirting precipices; a thousand causes of ruin beset and besiege him. The exquisite is a challenge thrown down to the possible. Nature aiming at the attainment of the highest animal type, can only succeed at the cost of such a birth being a crisis for the mother. If man had a head larger than that which he has in the more civilised races, he would kill his mother in being born; and he would be subject to perpetual congestions. Everything in nature is the result of a balance between advantages and disadvantages. The lever of the arm is very inconvenient for muscular effort; a better lever would have given us an arm like the wing of a pelican. Our heart, our spinal column, our brain, are very fragile things. Had they been more solid they would have been refractory to the delicate uses to which we put them. Nature never enters where there is no exit; to obtain the end which she pursues—always a good one—she goes on till the compensating inconvenience becomes deadly. She acts like a general who puts in the balance the importance of the object, and the losses requisite for its attainment. She desires the highest possible sum of life with the least possible suffering.

She desires,—no doubt I phrase the matter ill; but events fall out as though it were so. The definite result of the dark battle, which is being incessantly fought out, is in favour of righteousness. He that is too defective disappears or comes not into being; he that is imperfect reforms and aspires to be a possible type of normal life. This is so true that nature hardly disturbs herself about slight inconveniences. Even as it is easier in a commonwealth to correct great evils, ulcers that constitute a danger to life, than to extirpate little abuses that do not menace the existence of the body politic; so has nature left uncorrected in the human body faults that shock us, but which are not of a nature to condemn the species to impotence of existence.

HENRI-FRÉDÉRIC AMIEL.

[SECOND ARTICLE.]

AMIEL'S religion constantly tended to become more chastened; but it always remained a sad religion, as a whole more analogous to Buddhism than to Christianity. Although he finds fault with what he terms German Swaïsm, in Bahnsen for example, yet in reality he approaches very closely Hartmann's later formulæ. Sin and deliverance, these are in a word the whole theology of these modern disciples of Sakya-Mouni.

Nothing, in my view, can be more opposed to the ideas that ought to prevail in the future. What we ought to augment is the sum of happiness in human life. It is not of sin, of expiation, of redemption that henceforth we should speak to men; it is of kindliness, of gaiety, of indulgence, of good humour, of resignation. In proportion as hopes of a life beyond the tomb disappear, it is necessary to habituate men to look upon life as supportable; without that they will revolt against it. No longer is man to be maintained in peace by anything save happiness. But in a society of reasonably good structure very few persons have any reason to complain of having been put into the world. The cause of pessimism and nihilism is to be found in the ennui of a life which, by reason of a defective social organisation, is not worth the trouble of living. The value of life is only to be measured by its fruits; if we desire that men should hold fast to it, we must render it sweet and delectable.

Amiel asks himself with inquietude: "What is it that saves?" *Eh, mon Dieu!* It is precisely that which gives each man his motive in living. The way of salvation is not the same for all. For one man it is virtue, for another enthusiasm for truth, for yet another love of art, for others curiosity, ambition, travel, luxury, women, or wealth, in the lowest grade of all morphine and alcohol. Virtuous men find their reward in virtue itself; those who are not have pleasure.

All have imagination—that is to say, the highest joy of all, the enchantments that grow not old. Some cases of moral pathology apart, there is no life so sombre but that some ray of sunshine enters it still.

The most dangerous error with regard to social morality is the systematic suppression of pleasure. Rigorously severe virtue forms an aristocracy; every one is not equally drawn to it. He that has received the privilege of intellectual and moral nobility is under an obligation; but the good old Gaulois morality did not impose the same demands on all. Kindly feeling, courage and gaiety, and trust in the God of good people, suffice for salvation. The masses must be amused. For my own part, I do not experience any need for external amusement, but I require to feel that the people about me are being amused; I enjoy the gaiety of others. The temperance societies rest upon excellent intentions, but also upon a misunderstanding. I only know of one argument in their favour. Madame T. told me one day that in certain countries the married men, when they have not been temperate, beat their wives. Now that is horrible assuredly; we must try to correct it. But instead of suppressing drunkenness in those who have a need for it, would it not be better to attempt to render it sweet, amiable, and accompanied by the moral sentiments? There are so many men for whom the hours of drunkenness are, after the hours of love, the time when they are at their best!

Inequality and variety are the fundamental laws of the human species. There is nothing to suppress in the antagonistic manifestations of this strange collective being. It has been said that he is neither an angel nor a brute; I should prefer to say that he is at the same time an angel and a brute. An organised being eternal and perfect is a contradiction in terms. But for this reason are we to refuse the beam of light that nature affords us in our turn? It is as though we should spurn a cup of exquisite wine because it would be so soon exhausted, a pleasure because it does not endure. Inequality is great, no doubt; but nearly everybody has something, and the progress of human societies will reduce more and more the number of the disinherited. There remains pain, which indeed is a thing odious, humiliating, hurtful to the noble functions of life. But man can fight against it, almost suppress it, always endure it. The cases in which man is riveted to life are very rare. The only destiny absolutely condemned is that of the enslaved animal, of the horse for example, which cannot commit suicide, or indeed of the man sentenced to death and kept under surveillance, or the lunatic; but these are very exceptional cases. The immense majority of individuals have no need to complain of their passage through life, since the balance of life inclines to joy, and since painless death will doubtless come one day.

The problem of the origin of evil which so painfully exercised ancient philosophy is not then a problem at all. The Manichæan theory of the good God and the wicked God is irrefutable in the theistic conception of God as calculating and omnipotent. It has no longer any meaning in the conception of a universe spontaneously drawing from itself all that it can. Evil is the absolute condition of conscious existence. The world succeeds in procuring a little good, a little justice, and a little of the ideal with its myriads of egoisms. When one thinks of the road that must have been made, to permit Kant's theory of the categorical imperative to emerge from the system of reciprocal extermination which was the law of the primitive world, one is truly amazed at the wisely chosen paths that nature's policy has followed. The order of things in which evil has the greatest consequence, and in which our most sacred duty is to fight against it, is the human kingdom. Here, without contradiction, there is an infinity of work to be achieved; but it should be added that much has already been done. The world of humanity is to-day very much less wicked and very much less unjust than it was three or four thousand years ago. The general intention of the universe is benevolent. The evil still to be found existing in it is the necessary imperfection which spontaneity could not eliminate, and upon which it is the duty of science to make war. The question is to know whether—as M. Hartmann holds—the existence of the world is worse than the hypothesis of non-existence. For my own part, I believe that the hypothesis of existence is worth more, if only for the reason that it has been realised. The world, in M. Hartmann's opinion, is an effect without a cause. Existence, or at least consciousness, only commenced and only continues in the world because in existence there is a balance of good for conscious individuals as a whole.

A world in which evil predominated over good would be a world which either would not exist or would disappear. There are, in fact, very few beings who, brought face to face with destruction, do not hold it in horror. They prefer life with all its miseries to annihilation. Suicide is an extremely rare phenomenon. Even the creature that is, to all appearance, most odiously exploited by man has its compensations. The oyster gives pleasure to man, who swallows it under conditions which render its pain almost null; and for months before man has kept it in an oyster-bed, in which he has defended it against its enemies, and where it has enjoyed an existence longer and happier than it would have had in a state of nature. There are, we confess, some human beings for whom, by reason of fatal coincidences, it would be better not to be. Let us hope that cases of this kind will become more and more rare, and even disappear altogether.

Nothing, then, has less foundation than the objections made by the pessimists to the spirit of kindliness which, according to us, is dominant in the universe. Those objections pierce to the very heart pure theists, for whom the divine consciousness is a reflective consciousness scientifically combining things. They are insoluble for those who hold fast by the ideas of the old theology concerning the divine omnipotence. But such objections have no force against those who believe that the world is abandoned to the spontaneous action of its own forces. Nature is like a boiler at high pressure; she emits from herself all that the wall of the impossible does not hold in. In reality what the pessimists demand, what they conceive as the ideal of a perfect world, is a miraculous world, a world in which the *deus ex machina* would intervene unceasingly, to correct in detail the defects that he had been unable to detect in the mass. What possesses them above all is the anthropocentric error, the naïve fatuity of man judging the world from the point of view of his own comfort, as though the ant should adjust its theory of the universe by only taking into account the convenience of its little society.

Amiel has too much good sense to allow himself to follow out the exaggerations of the tactless school of thought that originated with the brilliant Schopenhauer. Amiel is a poet, and he has a warm love for nature. He half understands Goethe; then the fundamental contradiction of his being assumes the upper hand once more.

"Goethe ignores sanctity, and has never wished to reflect upon the terrible problem of evil. He never reached the feeling of obligation and of sin." This idealistic Manicheism is the more singular in Amiel in that he fully admits the claims of æsthetics. But the single fact of the admittance into nature of a species of coquetry is pregnant with consequence. If nature were evil, she would be ugly. Is it an effect of chance that the fundamental act of nature, the union of the sexes, is indissolubly bound to æsthetic feeling, and is in a sense the cause of all æsthetics? Beauty is the adornment that flower and animal put upon themselves with love in view. In this adornment of plant and animal there is never a fault in design, never a crude or ill-assorted colour. Nature must have taste; but she does not reach morality; she does not go beyond love.

That is why she is so often in the eyes of reason unjust and immoral. We feel an invincible need of supposing in the government of the world the justice which we find written upon our own hearts; and since it is perfectly evident that this justice has no existence in the reality of the universe, we come to absolutely exact as the condition of morality, the survival of each human consciousness beyond the tomb. Here the supreme antinomy between nature and reason bursts out. Such a postulate is, in fact, the most necessary *a priori* and the most impossible *a posteriori*. The thesis of the *Phædo* is nothing more than a subtilty. I greatly prefer the Judo-Christian system of the resurrection. The resurrection would be a miracle, and inconceivable in the actual state of things, where we behold nothing above material facts save this poor humanity still so feeble, and an obscure general consciousness wholly indifferent to individuals. Reason, moreover, is not omnipotent; it supports flagrant injustices which it is powerless to prevent. But were we to suppose that one day it should be omnipotent, nothing would then prevent it from being just, and retrospectively just to the ages in which justice had not been possible. In a word, God is already good, but he is not all-powerful. God, there can be no doubt, already does what he can for righteousness; one day, with the capital of the whole universe at his command, he will be able to do all. A great reparation might in this way be conceived; and, as a slumber of a million of ages is no longer than the slumber of an hour, the reign of justice that we have loved would appear to us as the immediate sequel of the hour of death.

Resurrection would be thus the final act of the world, the act of an all-powerful and all-knowing God, capable of being just and willing to be so. Immortality would not be as Plato wished it, an inherent quality of man, a consequence of his nature; it would be a gift reserved by the Being become absolute, perfect, omniscient, and omnipotent, for those who should have contributed to his development. It would be an exception, a divine selection, a recompense awarded by righteousness and truth in their triumph to the consciences of the past in which love of righteousness and truth had dominated, and to them alone. It would indeed be a miracle, that is to say, a divine premeditated act; such acts, of which at present we know not a single instance, would become the law of the universe on the day when the Being should have achieved perfect consciousness.

I sometimes try to imagine for myself a sermon suitable to All Saints' Day (the best remembered of holy days), to be delivered a thousand years hence, when it may be that a glimpse of the secret of immortality will have been vouchsafed. Is it not a remarkable thing that All Saints' Day, inseparable as it is from the Day of the Dead, should be the only holy day to which the people have clung? There is in the melancholy with which we think of the great and good men of ages less favoured than ours, a species of pious effort to give back life to them again. We must surely dream that all which has lived, still lives somewhere in an image capable of being reanimated. The stereotyped forms of all things are preserved. The stars at the further extremity of the universe are receiving, at this present hour, the image of events that have happened ages ago. The imprints of all that has existed still survive, ranged through the diverse zones of infinite space. It is for the supreme photographer to take new proofs. But he will only bring back to life once more that which has served the cause of righteousness, and consequently of truth. This will be our recompense. Inferior souls will have found theirs in the low enjoyments after which they have sought.

These are the questions which I should have liked so much to discuss with poor Amiel, had I had the pleasure of knowing him. On page 123 of the second volume I find that he does me a slight injustice. He is indignant because at times, in treating of these subjects, I give a place to humour and irony. Ah well! I do not think that there is anything unphilosophical in that. A complete darkness, perhaps providentially, hides from our eyes the moral ends of the universe. On this matter we lay odds and draw lots, in reality we know nothing. Our own particular wager, our *real acierto*, as the Spaniards say, is that the inward inspiration which makes us affirm duty is a sort of oracle, an infallible voice coming from without and corresponding to an objective reality. Into this persistent affirmation we put the nobler part of ourselves: we do well; we must hold fast by it, even in the face of evidence. But there are nearly as many chances for the contrary being true. It may be that these inner voices proceed from honest illusions nurtured by habit, and that the world may be no more than an amusing piece of enchantment, concerning which no god has any care. We must then bear ourselves in such a way, that in neither of the hypotheses we may be completely in error. We ought to give ear to the higher voices, but in such a manner that, in the case of the second hypothesis being the true one, we may not have been duped too greatly. If the world, in fact, be not a serious thing, it is the dogmatic people who will prove to have been frivolous, and the worldly people, those whom the theologians treat as thoughtless beings, who will have been the true sages.

In this way what appears to be advisable is a double-edged wisdom, equally prepared for either of the two eventualities of the dilemma, a middle path in which, one way or the other, we shall not have to say, *Ergo erravimus*. It is, above all, for others that we must be scrupulous. For one's self one can take great risks; but one has no right to play for other people. When we have souls in our keeping, we ought to express ourselves with sufficient reserve to ensure that, in the hypothesis of the great bankruptcy, those whom we have compromised should not be too greatly victimised.

In utrumque paratus! To be prepared for all contingencies, this perhaps is wisdom. To abandon one's self successively to confidence, scepticism, optimism, irony, —such is the means of being sure that, at least at moments, we have been in the right. You will tell me that this implies that one will never be completely right. No doubt; but as there is not the slightest chance of that combination being reserved for any one, it is prudent to fall back upon more modest pretensions. Ah well! the state of mind that M. Amiel disdainfully terms "the Epicureanism of the imagination" is not after all perhaps a bad part to take. Gaiety is so far very philosophical, in that it seems to say to nature that we do not take her any more seriously than she takes us; if the world be a bad farce, by gaiety we make it a good one. If, on the other hand, an indulgent and benevolent intelligence presides over the universe, we shall be far more fitted to enter into the intentions of this supreme intelligence by joyous resignation, than by the gloomy inflexibility of the sectary and the eternal jeremiad of the believer.

"Banter Pharisaism if you will, but speak straightforwardly to honest men," Amiel says to me with a certain asperity. *Mon Dieu!* How often honest men are Pharisees without knowing it! Socrates has the reputation of having invented irony. If that be true, it must be admitted that the Athenian sage said the last word in philosophy. We no longer, in fact, allow philosophy to be discussed otherwise than with a smile. We owe virtue indeed to the Eternal, but we have the right to add irony to it as a personal resumption. In this way we render, to whomever it is due, pleasantry for pleasantry, we take our turn in the game. St. Augustine's saying, *Domine, si error est a te decepti sumus*, remains a very fine one, thoroughly conforming to modern feeling. Only we desire that the Eternal should feel that if we accept the trickery, we accept it knowingly and willingly. We are resigned in advance to the loss of the interest on our virtuous investments, but we do not wish to be exposed to the ridicule of seeming to have counted too confidently on it.

Such was, besides, Amiel's own definite conclusion. Some weeks before his death he saw wisdom. Among the last leaves of the Journal there is a fine page that reads as follows :—

"For many years past the immanent God has had more actuality for me than the transcendent God, and the religion of Jacob has been more alien to me than that of Kant or even of Spinoza. The whole of the Semitic dramaturgy has come to appear to me as a work of imagination. The Apostolic writings have to my eyes changed in value and significance. Faith and truth have grown more and more sharply distinct from one another. Religious psychology has become a simple phenomenon, and has lost its fixed and noumenal value. The apologetics of Pascal, Leibnitz, and Secrétan appear to me to prove no more than those of the Middle Ages, for they presuppose that which is in question, a revealed doctrine, a definite and immutable Christianity. It seems to me that what remains to me from all my studies is a new phenomenology of mind, the intuition of universal metamorphosis. All private convictions, emotional principles, clearly defined formulæ, and infusible ideas are nothing more than prejudices, useful in practice but none the less manifestations of mental narrowness. The absolute in detail is absurd and contradictory. Political, religious, æsthetic, and literary factions are the anchyloses of thought. All special belief is an obstinacy and obtusity, but this consistency is at the proper time essential. Our monad, in so far as it is a thinker, overleaps the limits of time and space and historical surroundings; but in so far as it is an individual, and for purposes of action, it adapts itself to current illusions, and gives itself a determinate goal."

These lines were written on the 4th of February, 1881. Amiel died on the 11th of May in the same year. He had his failings, but his was one of the strongest speculative minds which from 1845 to 1880 reflected upon things. The form that he chose for the expression of his thought, a manuscript journal of 16,000 pages, was as disadvantageous as it well could be. Thanks to the posthumous care of his friends, thanks to M. Scherer, who in a profound study has given a perfect rendering of the beautiful character of his life, Amiel's thought will appear to all those who interest themselves in philosophic problems, as clearly and as completely as though he had known how to write a book—that is, to limit himself.

NOTES.

NOTES.

Note i., Page 14.

Chrétien de Troyes was a French poet who lived in the latter part of the twelfth century. The most celebrated of his poems —nearly all of which are based on the legends of the Round Table—is *Parceval le Gallois.* Little or nothing is known of his life.

Note ii., Page 14.

Wolfram of Eschenbach, the most famous of the *Minnesinger*, was born at Eschenbach, near Nuremberg, about the end of the twelfth century. He took a leading part in the "Poets' War," held by Hermann, Landgraf of Thuringia, in the Castle of Wartburg, 1207, and died about 1220. F. Schlegel calls him the greatest of German poets, and his works certainly show great imagination and power of expression. *Parsifal* and *Lohengrin*, owing to the use made of them by Wagner as subjects for his music-dramas, are his best known poems.

Note iii., Page 22.

Gervais of Tilbury was an English chronicler of the twelfth century, but appears to have spent most of his early life in Italy. He was a favourite of Henry II. and of the Emperor Otto IV. To the latter he dedicated *Otia Imperialia*, a curious collection of natural history, geography, politics, and folk-lore.

Note iv., Page 27.

Marco Kralevich is a half-mythical hero of Servian ballad-literature, in which his victories over the Turks and Magyars are narrated. He is at last killed on the battlefield, but the belief prevails that at his country's darkest hour he will appear again on earth and deliver Servia from her oppressors.

Note v., Page 42.

Giraldus Cambrensis is the name generally given to Girald de Barri, an historian and ecclesiastic, born about 1147, in Pembrokeshire. He was educated at the University of Paris, and became Archdeacon of St. David's. A journey to Ireland in 1185 gave him materials for his *Topographia Hiberniæ*. A few years later he wrote the *Itinerarium Cambriæ*. His writings are valuable for the insight they give into the political and social conditions of his time.

Note vi., Page 57.

Claudian, the last of the great Roman poets, lived in the end of the fourth and beginning of the fifth centuries, his principal work being an epic poem on the Rape of Proserpine. Procopius (to whom an essay is devoted in Renan's *Essais de Morale et de Critique*) was born about the end of the fifth century, and became the most eminent of the Byzantine historians. Johannes Tzetzes, a Greek poet and grammarian, was born at Constantinople about 1120 A.D., and died about 1183.

Note vii., Page 58.

The Bollandists were an association or rather succession of Jesuits, who issued (1643-1794) the *Acta Sanctorum*, a Series of Lives of the Saints. The name was derived from John Bolland, who edited the first five volumes.

Note viii, Page 65.

Gregory of Tours (540-594) was a French bishop and historian. His *History of the Franks* is the chief authority for the history of Gaul in the sixth century.

Note ix., Page 71.

The Beni-Israel ("Sons of Israel"), a curious settlement, evidently of Jewish origin, in different towns in the west of India, which is said to have existed for about a thousand years. The number of members is about five thousand, and marriage with other nationalities, or even ordinary Jews, rarely takes place.

Note x., Page 78.

Antiochus Epiphanes was king of Syria from 175 to 164 B.C. He conquered Egypt and twice took Jerusalem; but his attempts to force the worship of the Greek gods on the Jews caused the successful insurrection of Mattathias and the Maccabees.

Note xi., Page 91.

Alkindi (known to the Latin schoolmen as Alkindius) lived in the reigns of Al-Mamûn and Al-Motassem, and is said to have written two hundred treatises on scientific and philosophical subjects, only a few of which, however, have survived. Alfarabi (Alfarabius) died at Damascus in 950. According to legendary accounts he was a man of great learning, and knew seventy languages. "He gave the tone and direction to nearly all subsequent speculations among the Arabians." Avicenna (980-1037), by his medical and philosophical works, was the most illustrious of the oriental Arabic writers.

NOTE XII., PAGE 92.

Ibn Badja (Avempace) died at Fez in 1138. His principal work was an essay on the *Republic of the Solitary*. The same theme was developed by Ibn Tofail (Abubacer), who died at Marocco in 1185.

NOTE XIII., PAGE 92.

Bessarion (1395-1472) was one of the earliest of the scholars of the Renaissance. As Bishop of Nicæa in the Greek Church, he accompanied the Greek Emperor to Italy in 1439, in order to effect a union between the Eastern and Western Churches. On joining, soon after, the latter church, he was created a cardinal. Constantine Lascaris, a famous Greek scholar of the fifteenth century, was born at Constantinople; but on the capture of that city by the Turks in 1453, he sought asylum in Italy, where he lived till his death in 1493. He did much, both by teaching and writing, to revive the study of Greek.

NOTE XIV., PAGE 93.

Budé (Budeus) was born in 1467, and died in 1540. He wrote many Greek and Latin commentaries, was the most learned Frenchman of his time, and enjoyed the friendship of Erasmus. Lefèvre d'Étaples (1450-1537) was a scholar of great eminence, and a writer on theological and literary subjects.

NOTE XV., PAGE 93.

Gerbert, who afterwards became Pope Sylvester II., was born in Auvergne about 930. He pursued scientific studies among the Arabs in Spain, and is said to have introduced Arabic numerals and clocks into France. Constantine the African was a Carthaginian scholar of the eleventh century. He was said to have studied in Egypt and India, and wrote principally on medical subjects.

Note xvi., Page 95.

Ibn Khaldoun (1322-1406) was an Arabian historian, his chief work being a universal history which treats especially of the Arabs and Berbers.

Note xvii., Page 95.

Albateni (Albategnius), who was born in Mesopotamia about 850 and died in 929, was mainly noted for his astronomical and mathematical writings, including commentaries on Ptolemy.

Note xviii., Page 95.

Albertus Magnus (1193-1280) was one of the most distinguished of the scholastic philosophers and a member of the Dominican order. He studied at Padua and Bologna, taught theology and philosophy at Paris and Cologne, and was for a short time Bishop of Ratisbon. His fame chiefly rests on the fact that he was the first of the scholastics to reproduce Aristotle's philosophy, and transform it in accordance with Catholic dogma.

Note xix., Page 98.

Ali, born at Mecca about 600, killed at Kufa 661, was the adopted son of Mohammed and the fourth Caliph. The Shûte sect among the Mohammedans regard Ali with veneration as the first rightful Caliph.

Note xx., Page 99.

Avenzoar, an Arabian physician, was born in Spain about 1072 and died in 1162.. He was the teacher of Averroes, who spoke highly of his wisdom.

NOTE XXI., PAGE 114.

Hafiz was born at Shiraz in the beginning of the fourteenth century, and died between 1388 and 1394. He was a divine, a philosopher, a grammarian, and one of the greatest of the Persian poets.

NOTE XXII., PAGE 115.

The Caveau was a sort of Rhymers' Club which regularly met at the Café de Cancale. Founded in 1806 by Gouffé, Désaugiers, and others, it was a revival of the old Society of the Caveau, which had had a somewhat fitful existence since the early part of the eighteenth century. When Béranger first joined it in 1813, it had acquired considerable reputation both for its poetry and its wine, and published a monthly journal of its proceedings. Béranger's introduction to the Caveau is best told in his own words: "In 1813 there had existed for several years a society of song-writers and literary men, which had taken the name of *Caveau* in memory of the Caveau rendered illustrious by Piron, Panard, Collé, Gallet, and Crébillon, father and son. Désaugiers, on the death of old Laujon, had been elected president of this society, whose songs were in such singular contrast with the misfortunes then menacing France. I have never had much taste for literary associations, and I should never have had the idea myself of joining such a society. Désaugiers, who happened to see some verses of mine, sought my acquaintance, and I was unable to resist the invitations which he gave me to dine at least once at the Caveau with all his colleagues, whom I only knew by name. On the appointed day I duly went and sang many of my songs. Everybody was surprised that, considering the number of my productions, I should never have thought of publishing them. 'He must be one of us,' they all cried. In accordance with the rules which forbid the nomination of a candidate who is present, I was hidden behind the door with a biscuit and a glass of champagne. I improvised some verses of thanks for my election, which was carried unanimously to an accompaniment of clinking glasses and confirmed by a general embrace."--Béranger, *Ma Biographie.*

NOTE XXIII, PAGE 128.

Rutilius Claudius Numatianus was one of the later Roman poets. The date of his birth and death are unknown, but his principal poem, of which only 1700 lines are extant, dates from 416 A.D. It describes a coasting voyage from Rome to Gaul, and is filled with intense enthusiasm for Paganism and confidence in its future, accompanied by hatred of Christianity.

NOTE XXIV., PAGE 133.

Charles Forbes de Tryon, Comte de Montalambert (1810-1870), son of a French officer in the English service, was, at the outset of his career, one of the followers of Lamennais in his attempts to combine democracy and catholicism. He afterwards became a leader of the Ultramontane party. Renan refers to his *Life of St. Elizabeth of Hungary*, published in 1836.

NOTE XXV., PAGE 162.

Jean Colerus, the biographer of Spinoza, was a Protestant pastor at the Hague.

NOTE XXVI., PAGE 163.

Friedrich Heinrich Jacobi (1743-1819) was a German statesman, philosopher, and man of letters. He corresponded with Goethe, and engaged in controversies with Moses Mendelssohn and Schelling. He has been called the founder of the "Philosophy of Faith."

NOTE XXVII., PAGE 166.

Moses Maimonides (1135-1204?), a celebrated Jewish rabbi of the Middle Ages, was born at Cordova. He studied under Averroes, but was at last driven by persecution to Egypt, where he died. His best known work was the *Guide to the Perplexed*, a theological work which raised some controversy among orthodox Jews.

NOTE XXVIII., PAGE 166.

Cosmas Indicopleustes lived in the sixth century. He was an Egyptian monk and traveller, and was the author of a book on geography and theology called *Topographia Christiana.*

NOTE XXIX., PAGE 166.

Uriel Acosta, a Portuguese Jew of noble family, was born about 1594. He was brought up as a Catholic, but adopted Judaism, and fled to Amsterdam to avoid persecution. His *Examinations of Pharisaic Traditions* (1624) caused his co-religionists to persecute him as an atheist. He was deprived of his property, twice excommunicated, and compelled to undergo penance. After writing a remarkable autobiography, entitled *Exemplar humanæ vitæ*, he at last shot himself in 1647.

NOTE XXX., PAGE 168.

The College of the Sorbonne was founded about 1250 by Robert de Sorbonne, confessor of Louis IX. It became the seat of the theological faculty in the University of Paris, and exercised much influence in ecclesiastical affairs, especially in the sixteenth and seventeenth centuries.

Note xxxi., Page 168.

Henry Oldenburg (1626-78) was a native of Bremen, but spent most of his life in England. He was one of the first members of the Royal Society, and maintained an extensive correspondence with Spinoza, Leibnitz, Bayle, and others of his learned contemporaries. Milton addresses him in his *Epistolæ Familiares.*

Note xxxii., Page 173.

Richard Simon was born at Dieppe, 1638, and died there 1712. He published several works on biblical criticism, one of which, a *Critical History of the Old Testament*, was suppressed in France, but published in Holland, 1685.

Note xxxiii., Page 180.

Lucilio Vanini was born at Taurisano in 1585, and took orders as a priest. His studies in physical science and the learning of the Renaissance however caused him to forsake the Church. After sojourning in France, Switzerland, the Low Countries, and England, and constantly suffering persecution for his heretical opinions, he was executed at Toulouse, with revolting cruelty, in 1619. His *Amphitheatrum Æternæ Providentiæ* and *De Amirandis Naturæ Arcanis* make it clear that his teaching was pantheistic in tendency. See Owen's *Skeptics of the Italian Renaissance.*

Note xxxiv., Page 192.

Raymond Lully (1235-1315) was a Spanish scholastic and alchemist, and a missionary to the Mohammedans. He was the author of a system of Logic called *Ars Magna*, and of many other works.

NOTE XXXV., PAGE 196.

Philipp Konrad Marheineke (1780-1846) was a German Protestant theologian and church historian, and became professor in several universities, including that of Berlin. His principal work was a *History of the German Reformation.*

NOTE XXXVI., PAGE 198.

Jules Lachelier, a modern French writer on philosophy, was born in 1832. While he has written little, his influence in France as a follower of Kant has been considerable.